The Christian Initiation of Children

Hope for the Future

Robert D. Duggan
and
Maureen A. Kelly

PAULIST PRESS

New York/Mahwah

Library of Congress Cataloging in Publication Data

Duggan, Robert D.
     The Christian initiation of children : hope for the future /
Robert D. Duggan and Maureen A. Kelly.
          p.   cm.
     Includes bibliographical references.
     ISBN 0-8091-3258-3
     1. Catholic Church—Education—United States. 2. Initiation
rites—Religious aspects—Catholic Church. 3. Christian education
of children. 4. Christian education of young people. 5. Christian
education—Philosophy. I. Kelly, Maureen A., 1942-   . II. Title.
BX926.D84   1991
268'.8273—dc20
                                                             90-25973
                                                                  CIP

Published by Paulist Press
997 Macarthur Blvd.
Mahwah, New Jersey 07430

Printed and Bound in the United States of America.

Contents

Introduction   1

1. A New Era   11

2. Christian Initiation   25

3. Liturgical Rites   47

4. A Suitable Pastoral Formation   69

5. Conversion that Is Personal and Developed   89

6. Within the Community of the Faithful   112

Annotated Table of Contents   133

Introduction

This is a radical book. It contains a radical vision which challenges much of what we have come to take for granted about how the Christian experience should be passed on to the next generation. Like any truly radical set of ideas, the vision articulated here draws from the taproot of Christian experience. As such, it springs from what is primordial and foundational about Christian belief, and thus is free from the overlay of custom, routine, and caution.

Besides being radical, this book is also meant to be a practical and helpful tool for individuals, parish staffs, and committees. It is the hope of the authors that readers will use the questions and activities presented at the end of each chapter to both envision and begin to implement more meaningful and effective policies and structures for the initiation of children into our Catholic faith community.

The vision of this book is about how we—and in particular our young people—come to be believers in Jesus whom we proclaim to be the Christ. It is about initiation, the most basic task of the Christian community; it is about sharing with others a life-transforming and world-changing experience of encounter with God, revealed in the gracious love of Jesus. Specifically, this book is about how one generation best passes on to the next all that it has come to learn about faith in the God of Jesus and in the church which mediates a divine presence in our midst. The radical nature of what follows involves a challenge to our conventional wisdom governing the why's and wherefore's of current religious formation efforts with children.

Our starting point is an admission of failure. We want to shout, "The emperor has no clothes!" to all who have grown complacent with or chosen to ignore what is happening with our children's religious education across the country. We want to force an admission that *it's just not working* from all who would choose denial as the more comfortable option when surveying the landscape of religious education for the young.

With the admission of failure there is sometimes a tendency to lay blame on content, method or materials in religious education. It is not the intention of this book to make religious education the scapegoat for our present failures. People who would do this usually have an image of formal religious instruction/education as the whole of the catechetical endeavor. It is only a part. Furthermore, it is a part that cannot stand on its own. A good textbook, a well-trained catechist or religion teacher, and a group of the best children in the world are not enough to accomplish the task we are about in Christian formation.

Our admission of failure stems from our experience of youngsters arriving for first eucharist interviews who do not even know the Our Father, or who know the Our Father and other prayers, but cannot remember the last time they went to Mass. Our admission of failure comes in a perverse irony worth contemplating: many young people undergo their first alienating experience of church in the ritual performed by a grumpy priest who feels keenly the foolishness of mandatory confession for seven- and eight-year-olds, but is unwilling to risk episcopal wrath should he allow the children to forego the sacrament or celebrate it in a meaningful communal ritual. Real failure is sensed when first confession becomes the only confession, and high school students are heard to say, "I think I got that one when I was little." Admission of failure comes when one sees the fear and anger felt by many people over the debate about the age for confirmation and the differing theologies of confirmation, and then realizes that much of that fear comes from their knowledge that for a large portion of young people this will be the sacrament of exit from the church.

With all of our research and rhetoric on adult education and faith development, we must admit failure when religious educators use "sacramental preparation programs" as coercive tools to force unchurched or reluctant parents into assuming their "rights" as primary educators of their children, all the while knowing that the parents are operating out of such diverse levels of faith and knowledge of the Christian tradition that the sessions are almost guaranteed to miss most of the people most of the time. What contribution such sessions actually make to the children's appreciation of the Christian message is virtually impossible to discern.

As if this disarray were not enough, the whole question of religious education has been politicized and exploited by ideologies of every hue. The religious right wing continues to spend enormous energy scouring scope and sequence charts to ensure that adequate doctrine is poured into Judy and Johnny's heads; and the liberal left is so unsure of its stance and identity as a church that it doesn't want to teach something that might change in the next generation anyway. The hierarchy decrees the failure of the experiential method of catechesis and extols a return to the catechism, and bewildered parents and catechists retreat into helplessness and (for some) hopelessness.

Is it not high time that we address the emperor's nakedness? That child's tale of ambition, greed, deceit, pride, and human respect does, after all, have a moral lesson to impart. It is confrontation with the truth, no matter how disconcerting or embarrassing, that is finally redemptive for the emperor as well as for the citizenry of the kingdom. A long, hard look at the way things are and a willingness to admit the shocking sight we behold are the first steps toward change for the better.

Our reading of these phenomena is that the present generation is presiding over the death throes of one era and the birth pangs of another. If there is reason for grieving the loss of what once seemed to "work" but clearly no longer does, there is just as much reason for hope as we read the signs of the new beginning of which we are also a part. The hopeful vision of this book rests on the promise of that new beginning. It is our conviction that we are already able to discern and describe the contours of that fresh start, and that it offers us hope for a new Pentecost. Forces of renewal in the church have already made clear some basic directions, have already retrieved from our heritage precious treasures that have proven to be life-giving. We need to trust the outlines of that hopeful future emerging from the renewal set in motion by the Second Vatican Council.

It is possible to describe a better way of leading our children into an experience of Christian faith. We use the word *initiation* rather than *education* to describe this process, because it seems to convey better and with less negative connotation the task that is ours. We see weeds that still grow among the wheat; but there is a new growth already bearing rich fruit in the church of Vatican II. The vision of children's initiation developed in this book is drawn from those roots that have proven most life-giving and hope-filled in today's church. We recognize where that new growth has borne fruit in revitalized communities and see there the movement of the Spirit. We discern the power unleashed in personal and communal conversion experiences, and we recognize the fire of a new Pentecost which must be shared with the next generation.

A major source of the radical vision which informs this book is the sweeping revitalization of parishes that has occurred when they have taken seriously the implementation of the *Order of Christian Initiation of Adults* (RCIA).[1] At once extremely conservative and traditional, yet forward-looking and progressive, the *Order* has proven to be one of the most dramatic "surprises" of the Second Vatican Council. Its blend of theological and pastoral insight, its renewed ecclesiology, its implicit and explicit priorities in the areas of faith, witness and service, its structures enabling empowerment for ministry based on baptismal call, its insistence on conversion to gospel values as the church's primary agenda— all of this and more have given incredible impetus to communities that have embraced the challenge of the *Order*.

We believe that the *Order* in its assumptions and

underlying theology has much to say about a way out of the morass we experience in parish life and practice today. It is so different from what we are used to that as people begin to implement the *Order* in a parish they often have the experience of a child with a kaleidoscope as various pieces float around and are separated. An impatient child or one who is prone to immediate satisfaction might very well put the kaleidoscope down and move to an orderly diversion. The patient, curious child continues the experience until a whole picture is formed. It is out of the latter type of experience that our claim is made that the *Order* provides us with a "missing piece" which fills in the puzzle.

This book is not about adapting an RCIA model for everything in parish life. Rather, it is about taking a long, hard look at a missing but newly found piece of initiation—and all that this implies—and then working it through to new and different structures and practices in the parish's initiation of pre-adolescent young people and their families. Without the initiation piece, we have had the cart before the horse, particularly in religious education. We have educated and informed, hoping that initiation and conversion would happen. This book seeks to be intentional about initiation and conversion in parishes, recognizing that our children are the hope of the future.

Our excitement over the new era of human history of which we are a part stems in large measure from the conviction that we are now poised to make the most of gathering forces for renewal which have yet to be unleashed in their fullness. Now is the time to lead our children into a new era of the church's life. Now is the time to shape their Christian experience in ways that are as decisively new as the age which dawns with the twenty-first century. Now is the time to abandon the old pedagogical model and to begin to initiate our children into the power of Jesus Christ for the life of the world. That new Pentecost will bring about an excitement for the Christian way of life that will rival the triumphant song of the martyrs marching to glory in the arena.

Our generation stands at a fork in the road. As few eras before us, ours is an age able to choose its destiny. What could be more crucial than the effort to form our children in a faith that will be up to the challenge of the new era which dawns? If we dare to begin initiating our children in the ways described in this volume, they—and we, and our world—will never be the same again.

Questions for Group Discussion

1. What are the signs or symptoms in your parish that indicate the present way of approaching children's religious education is not working?

2. What part of the Introduction most resonated with your experiences?

3. List the ways your parish prepares children for sacraments.

What is asked of parents?

What is asked of children?

What is asked of the worshiping community?

Note

1. The popular term RCIA (Rite of Christian Initiation of Adults) is misleading. The official Latin document is called an *Ordo*, since it contains a number of rites, both for children of catechetical age and for adults. We use the term *Order* in this work because it is a more accurate rendering of the Latin text and because it evokes the fuller ecclesiological and theological content implied in the notion of an "*ordo.*"

1. A New Era

It should come as no surprise to any thoughtful person that the enterprise of religious education is undergoing a time of turbulence. Social commentators and cultural critics have observed in some detail the unprecedented speed of change that has characterized our century, and the repercussions which rapid change have meant in nearly every field of human activity are familiar to all of us.

Parish ministers regularly experience these huge changes in micro-cosmic symptoms, and they then ask questions such as: What do you do when . . .

—parents don't set religious education as a priority?

—a child baptized in two traditions goes to both the church of the father and church of the mother, and wants to receive eucharist in one or both?

—you teach about the church's view on marriage and 75 percent of the children in your class have experienced divorce in their own nuclear family?

—sports and extra-curricular activities take precedence over church?

—people don't have time to do volunteer catechetical ministry?

—you know children are more evangelized into the story, values and models of the advertising media than the Christian tradition?

—you have done all the "right" things in setting up religious education programs and sacramental processes, but there are no visible results once they are over?

"THE GOOD OLD DAYS"

In the strong ethnic communities populated by the immigrant populations of the United States well into the first half of this century, the church served a crucial role in helping people maintain their distinctive identity which was threatened with assimilation into the larger culture on many levels. The strong communal bonds of each successive minority group were reinforced by customs, traditions and family rituals which were of a piece with the religious faith they professed. In that context, the rigid sort of indoctrination which passed for religious education "worked" because it was part of a larger set of initiatory processes that surrounded a child from infancy to adulthood.

The secularization of our society which has become so marked in the second half of the twentieth century has coincided with the breakdown of those strong ethnic communities and the assimilation of many distinctive cultures into the great American melting pot. Religiously, this has been an even more intense period of upheaval for Roman Catholics because of the vast changes which our church has undergone as a result of Vatican II's call for renewal. Not surprisingly, the disappearance of "ghetto Catholicism" has had profound implications for our ability to transmit effectively the riches of Catholic culture and faith to the young of today. The revolution which has occurred in religious education in the last thirty years is the result of the breakdown of that larger Catholic world which had been the bearer of faith so successfully for centuries.

In local American parishes of the first half of the twentieth century, there was a strong, consistent context for initiation and conversion which was supported by religious instruction. Characteristic of that context was the presence of believing, practicing adults—usually two generations—who were in close proximity to children. These adults shared faith with children in many day-to-day informal settings; and whether it was parent, grandparent, or peer, the language of explanation was invariably the same. Parish life was part and parcel of family life. Parish was where extended families went not only for spiritual nourishment but also for social support. Church was the place to be somebody. Coupled with that, in strong ethnic neighborhoods there was a style of personal devotion and ritual activity which sprang out of one's native cultural heritage.

The explosive growth of communications technologies and the arrival of the mass media into everyone's home signaled the end of control over narrow and consistent cultural messages in families, neighborhoods, and churches. The mass media brought new ways of thinking and modeling, new values and lifestyles to old and young. The consequences of this change have been far-reaching because now the same cultural messages are presented to people regardless of age, race, ethnicity, religious persuasion, or socio-economic status. Families have become more mobile as corporations and big business have replaced small neighborhood and local government jobs. As a result, consistent intergenerational groupings for "traditioning" children have broken down. In a sense, what has happened and continues to occur is that more institutions are competing today for the faith of children and adults than ever before. More institutions and communities proffer answers to the basic human questions: Who am I? What will make me happy and valuable?

Stable worlds and world views were shattered in a very short period of time during the second half of the twentieth century. At the same time, in the area of religious education, two very positive trends emerged. The first was the incorporation of human experience into the content, method, and structure of religious education. The second was a new emphasis on the importance of adult religious education. What was missed, however, was the realization that the changes happening in the world were much more complex and would have more far-reaching, radical effects on children, on adults, and on the church than anyone could have suspected.

SHOOTING THE RAPIDS OF CHANGE

In his book, *Structure of Scientific Revolutions*, Thomas S. Kuhn has shown how new ways of understanding and experiencing the world rarely come about in peaceful, orderly fashion. New information, new situations and experiences disrupt the old synthesis until it simply collapses and ushers in a "paradigm shift" which involves whole new ways of thinking and acting. Given the massive cultural and social change of the twentieth century, how could anyone be surprised at our society's need to re-define a host of its basic tasks? The role and function of our culture's basic units, from family structure to relations between the sexes, from educational institutions to the role of government in our private lives, all of these and more have been called into question, have been subjected to intense scrutiny and debate, and have, without exception, undergone massive change. The reactions are predictable and understandable: fear, disbelief, anger, a sense of betrayal and disorientation, hopelessness, outrage.

Historically, in time of upheaval, society has generally turned to its religious institutions as a bulwark against the chaos which threatened to overwhelm it. In the second half of the twentieth century this has not always proven feasible. Without the supportive influences of a cohesive Catholic culture, religious educators of the young have been left with an impossible task. Training in religious literacy, which previously had been so valuable a part of the church's effort to indoctrinate its young, clearly no longer works. The failure to which we pointed in the Introduction is largely a reflection of the inability of religious education—whether it be the "new catechetics" or a nostalgic return to the *Baltimore Catechism*—to accomplish on its own what never should have been its sole responsibility.

In many ways, the fury which has surrounded the religious education of Catholic children in recent years has been misdirected. The issue is not whether Catholic schools should survive nor whether the CCD program is teaching Johnny the basics of our faith. The Catholic right's obsession with ensuring that catechetical materials have the full content of orthodox faith misses the mark by a mile. So, too, does the liberal left miss the point in pouring all of its energies into an uncritical acceptance of every new idea simply because it is new and different. The ravings of those at either end of the ideological spectrum, and the bewildered silence of those in between, look more like the dysfunctional patterns of a traumatized family system than a prayerful community of faith asking what is really best for the children. Scapegoating, whether it comes from the conservative or the liberal, remains a pattern of behavior that is unhealthy and ultimately ineffective.

The "problem" does not lie with a particular textbook series, nor with any particular catechetical methodologies. Rather, it is that we have asked too much from too few, and too little from too many. Too much from too few, in that we have expected religious education to carry a burden which properly belongs to the church at large. And too little from too many, in that we have failed to call on the entire Catholic community to become involved in the enormous challenge of passing on to our children an ancient heritage of faith in an era of dramatic social, cultural, political, economic, and religious change. The problem, or better, the challenge, is to create a new synthesis of faith and life that will invigorate today's children with a Catholic vision that not only helps them make personal sense of their lives, but also enables them to become effective in shaping a better world in the next millennium. Commentators who have recently suggested that this is the "Catholic moment" only serve to remind us of the urgency of our task.

The authors of this volume write from the deep conviction that as a church we are "up to" meeting this challenge. We believe strongly that the prayer for a "new Pentecost" in our church which Pope

John XXIII asked us to make for the success of the Vatican Council has indeed been heard. We have received an unprecedented call to be a church in change, not retreating to the security of the accustomed and familiar, but leading the way to discover new ways of being church in the midst of an evolving world. No generation in the history of the Christian tradition has dared to do what ours has done: revamp completely its entire symbol-system, from the signs and symbols of liturgical ritual to the theological language and formulations of cherished belief. Cultural anthropologists who know the extremely conservative nature of religious systems have looked in awe at the way in which our church has managed the reforms of Vatican II. The miracle, from their perspective, is not just that we should have made the attempt, but that we have accomplished so much without massive defection and catastrophic consequences.

The bark of Peter, it seems, is shooting the rapids of cultural change. It is just wishful thinking to believe that we can slow its speed or pause along the way to get our bearings. What we most need are skilled helmsmen who can avoid the danger spots and are willing to push forward fearlessly to the calmer waters that lie ahead. Ours is indeed a new era of human history. Even if there were some truth to the myth of "the good old days," there is simply no going back to them. The attempts of those who seek a return to the values and styles of previous generations are inevitably *new* attempts, in a new context, that bear only faint resemblance to the remembered models of the past.

The mandate of Vatican II to discern the "signs of the times" (*Gaudium et Spes* 4) requires of us a careful reading of our situation. Unlike so many other segments of our culture, we Catholics are able to do this from the vantage point of a rich and highly differentiated religious tradition. The intellectual and cultural heritage that is ours in the church is an enormous asset as we try to sort out what of the new is of value and what is to be discarded or adapted.

Our church has been gifted throughout this time of change with critical thinkers who have been able to analyze and reflect on what is happening about them, and even to discern future courses and directions. History will very likely look upon the church of Vatican II as one specially endowed with thinkers up to the task of renewal. The great minds of Karl Rahner, Teilhard de Chardin, Bernard Lonergan and others who were able to explain and chart the course of change have equipped us well for the task at hand.

The Vatican Council itself identified a renewed liturgy as the primary source whence would come the revitalized Christian experience for which we prayed. The heart of the liturgical renewal mandated at the council has come to us in the new way that we are called to celebrate the Christian sacraments of initiation. Within the space of a few short years, the

Roman Catholic Church issued entirely new rituals for infant baptism, adult initiation, confirmation and eucharist. One cannot help but recognize a providential convergence between the church's renewal of its initiatory praxis and the demands—both in our own country and in countless other cultures around the world—for an experience of Christian faith that is authentic, vital, and full of promise for global transformation. If some would see this as a Catholic moment in America, we would say that the cutting edge of a renewed Catholicism around the world lies in the dramatic step taken at Vatican II to alter and renew the way in which we initiate both children and adults into the community of believers.

Now, the post-Vatican II church must do as effective a job in its time as did the post-Tridentine church in its efforts to accomplish a Catholic Counter-Reformation. We have the advantage of history to show us how successful was the Tridentine synthesis in accomplishing its goals. For ourselves, we require a prophet's eye to discern how best to seize our moment in history and engage in the task of renewal given us at Vatican II.

The generation of believers immediately after Trent set to work promulgating a vision of renewal in several ways, but especially by creating the *Roman Catechism* (progenitor of the *Baltimore Catechism* more familiar to us) and then working to ensure its widespread use among succeeding generations. Although some today would hope for a similar tool, the Vatican Council itself was more visionary. It opted instead to create liturgical/sacramental structures of pastoral formation that would put us in touch with the ancient wellsprings of a vital Christian experience of faith. In the Council's document on liturgical renewal, *Sacrosanctum Concilium* (SC), and in *Ad Gentes*, the document on the missionary nature of the church, a vision of evangelization, catechumenal formation, and liturgical celebration was elaborated as the privileged way to revitalize the church's initiatory efforts. This renewal has been given flesh in magisterial documents of the past twenty-five years which have gradually elaborated the council's vision. Documents of liturgical reform from the Concilium and subsequent Roman congregations, as well as papal encyclicals, episcopal synods, and lesser documents from various departments of the Holy See and individual episcopal conferences around the world have sought to implement the council's mandates in ways faithful to the Spirit-led vision of Vatican II.

A NEW TASK FOR A NEW ERA

It is important to keep this broad context in mind as we focus on our specific concern for the initiation of children into our Catholic faith and way of life. The thoughts developed in this chapter are meant to illuminate this context in a way that will frame our discussion more clearly and more helpfully. In the new era of which we are a part, the way our church calls its children to faith must reflect accurately the social, cultural, and religious contexts of the world in which they live, or else we will be dismissed as irrelevant.

Above all, it should be obvious by now that the pastoral challenge we face with our children is the result of a paradigm shift of massive proportions. The authors' shorthand way of referring to that shift is to say that our task today is one of initiation rather than religious education or religious literacy training. Christian initiation, with our children as well as with adults, is the agenda set before us.

In a secularized society, in what some would call a post-Christian era, in a world of incredible change, we are called to move into new ways of thinking and acting that will initiate children into the ancient yet ever-new faith of our ancestors. The "Copernican revolution" which Karl Rahner described in a theological context comes to pass with surprising speed at the parochial level in very practical, pastoral ways as we begin to understand the demands placed on us in the ministry of Christian initiation.

The object of this volume is to describe how Christian initiation must be done with our children if we are to meet successfully the challenge given us. Subsequent chapters will explore in some detail how specific elements of that initiatory vision can operate in a parish setting.

Questions for Group Discussion

1. In the last twenty years, in what ways has your parish responded to the changes in religious education? Be specific.

What do you see as the results, both positive and negative?

2. In overall programming and processes, how has your parish responded to what the authors have described as a "new era"?

What other possible responses can you envision?

3. "More institutions and communities proffer answers to the basic human questions: Who am I? What will make me happy and valuable?"

a. In your own local situation, what institutions and communities compete with the church for the "commitment" of families/adults and/or children? List them.

b. Consider those listed as "evangelizers" and describe their methods of welcome and invitation, their promise, their means of motivation and participation. What kind of commitment do they ask of participants?

c. From what you have listed and described, what insights have you gleaned about your own parish's evangelizing processes?

d. What could you begin to do differently with regard to your families and children? Your worshiping community?

2. Christian Initiation

Initiation means to begin or start. It also means to admit a person by special forms or ceremonies into the mysterious, secret knowledge of a community. To be initiated in the second sense presupposes there is a community which holds within itself a mystery, or a special knowledge. The *Order of Christian Initiation* assumes, as well it should, that the church is such a community.

Any kind of initiation has to do with a process of being absorbed into and bonded to a group. Initiates put on a new identity. They gradually develop a sense of belonging. The stories, traditions and values of the group, whether that group is a family, a sports community, a fraternity or a church, become "mine" through a process of initiation. In any context, initiation has as its goal to make and form individuals and communities who are committed to the history, symbols, values and celebration of the group. A community committed to the work of initiation expects conversion to its "way of life" as a basic criterion for membership. Examples abound in our experience. Families initiate future in-laws. Ethnic communities start with the very young. College fraternities and sororities demand some-times life-threatening initiation activities. Sports communities seduce (evangelize) with symbols and rites so robust and clear that even the non-initiated get caught up in them.

Each of these communities holds a story that is of such value to its members that they want to share it. All of their celebrations take hold of the initiate as he/she participates in them. None of these commu-nities is content to rest if the person being initiated still wants to be a member in name only. They all, at some level, want disciples who are committed mem-bers. Not one of these communities would take seri-ously a request to join but not participate. Imagine the prospective in-law who will not come to dinner to meet the family, the college student who will pay dues but not attend the fraternity gatherings, the faithful football fan who does not recognize the col-ors of the home team.

When an authentic initiation process occurs for an individual, the values, symbols and ethical behavior of the group are internalized. One never thinks of "graduating" from an initiatory communi-ty. One may perhaps leave by choice, or become less engaged, but one does not become initiated in order to finish.

LOSS OF PERSPECTIVE

In our present-day pastoral experience, examples of the loss of an initiatory perspective abound. How often have we heard remarks such as these:

—What if they (the children) don't get "it" (everything about Roman Catholicism) before eighth grade?

—If we move confirmation to a younger age, we'll never see them again.

—Maybe we should go ahead and baptize or celebrate first eucharist with this child, even though we know she will rarely be able to celebrate the eucharist with us, because no one will bring her back to church.

—If we just had a lesson every year on the Mass . . . or reconciliation . . . or abortion . . ., then "they" would know . . . (whatever it is we're most concerned about at the moment).

The irony of these situations and many others is that they show so clearly that we really don't expect to initiate, nor do we really assume conversion. We educate, inform and hope. . . . We put the cart before the horse.

We can gain better access to how Christian initiation of children or adults operates when we look to other familiar models of initiation. How do children come to belong and commit to their family of origin, to its story, values, models, vision, celebration, and ethical behavior? The adults around them "tradition" them: tell them stories, do things with them, repeat the lessons over and over, welcome them into the family rituals and make them active participants. How do children become initiated into the American sports community, or music, or cults? Reflection by the reader on these phenomena will help to make many connections with secular initiatory contexts and should bring to the fore many things we have lost sight of in our ministry with children.

A RENEWED VISION OF INITIATION

In the remainder of the present chapter, we will sketch out in summary form the basic contours of a renewed initiatory vision. There are many sources from which we might draw in elaborating this vision. The church has been prolific in issuing guiding documents since the Vatican Council, and there is a wealth of theological reflection available based on pastoral experience of the past several decades. From these many possibilities, we choose to draw especially from the *Order of Christian Initiation of Adults*. Given our focus on children, the choice could seem questionable. Why is this source chosen above others to articulate a basic vision of children's initiation?

The RCIA, as the *Order* is popularly called, holds a privileged place in shaping the church's initiatory vision because of its nature as a liturgical document. As a *locus theologicus* (i.e., a source for theological reflection), the church's liturgical experience has always enjoyed a claim to primacy. Vatican

II called the liturgy "source and summit" of faith, thus capturing succinctly the wisdom of centuries of Christian experience in this regard. If one wishes to find the church's most authentic vision of initiation, where better to turn than to the document which sets the basic liturgical, theological and pastoral framework for our generation? Despite the appearance of "adult" in its title, the *Order* also governs how initiation is to be done for children of catechetical age who were not baptized as infants. Those who, although baptized as infants, were never catechized but now seek to complete their initiation through confirmation and first eucharist are also included explicitly in the *Order*'s directives. It is not much of a leap, and in fact is a step the authors wish to take, to recognize the applicability of much of the *Order*'s initiatory vision to those children in a parish who were baptized as infants and are in the regular course of catechesis. Even the *Order* cites the viability of combining into peer groups ("companion groups") the children seeking full initiation (baptism, confirmation, eucharist) and those already baptized and pursuing the usual pattern of pastoral formation as part of parish life (254.1). The *Order* envisions this involvement of already baptized children from the parish in the initiatory process as extending not just to catechetical sessions, but also to joint celebrations of the sacraments of initiation (256, 308).

As we gradually have come to understand that our responsibility for *all* our children is initiation, not just religious education, the *Order* has become an increasingly important source for understanding how we are called to make radical changes in the way our parishes deal with children across the board. The insistence of the *Order* on the integrity of the three sacraments of initiation (baptism, confirmation, eucharist) which must be celebrated in that sequence at a single celebration has made more and more people question the confused sacramental sequence (baptism-penance-eucharist-confirmation) which has become familiar only in this century. This is but one of the more obvious ways that the impact of the initiatory vision of the *Order* is being felt parish-wide, and not just among a few children seeking baptism.

In sketching out how the *Order* understands the initiation of children, we want to make clear our contention that this is a vision which should inform our pastoral care for all of our children, not just the unbaptized. The *Order* has transformed entire parishes where the adult rite is fully implemented. Similarly, where communities embrace its vision of initiation for certain groups of children, parishes will see a transformation in the way all of the children are formed in the faith.

As children's catechumenates flourish in more and more parishes, traditional structures of religious education will give way before an initiatory praxis that is clearly more vital, more effective and more consistent with the needs of our age.

INITIATION: THE COMMUNITY'S RESPONSIBILITY

How, then, might we summarize the understanding of Christian initiation, and specifically the initiation of children, which is embodied in the *Order*? One of the most fundamental insights offered by the *Order* is that initiation is the responsibility of the entire community, not just a specialized task to be done by one segment of a parish (e.g., religious educators). The *Order* insists that initiation "takes place within the community of the faithful" (4) and that it "is the responsibility of the baptized . . . hence, the entire community must help the candidates and the catechumens throughout the process of initiation" (9). Lest anyone take these admonitions as mere rhetoric, the document proceeds to spell out the various responsibilities of every segment of the parish, from the community at large and the assembly gathered for worship, to the individual ministries that assist in particular ways (catechists, presiders, godparents, and so forth).

There is a reason, intrinsic to the nature of initiation, why it is essential for the entire community to own its responsibility for the success of the process. Initiation has to do with a community's efforts to reconstitute itself in every new generation by passing on its constitutive stories, symbols, values, and traditions.

Our age of specialization and compartmentalization easily forgets the basic truth of this vision. The whole community in all its parts must be deeply committed to the work of initiation, or else what is transmitted to the next generation is a truncated set of experiences, lacking wholeness and balance, inevitably distorted by the absence of those who fail to contribute their gifts to the process.

In its insistence on the communal nature of the initiation process, the *Order* is articulating an ecclesiology as well as a common wisdom that has emerged from the experience of virtually every human society. By further specifying how this process operates in a series of overlapping contexts (these are identified as ministries), the *Order* reminds us that a child's initiation occurs within a network of communities. The family, of course, is the child's primary community. Theologically, we hold this because of our belief in the family as domestic church. But even sociologically and as an anthropological given, we recognize the decisive role of the family as primary vehicle for the initiation of a child into every level of human community.

In subsequent chapters we will make clear some of the implications of these insights for an initiatory praxis with children that is family-centered and inter-generational. Parishes of the future, if they are to be faithful to this vision of initiation, will have to develop strategies and structures that facilitate a child's initiation into the Christian faith with maximum involvement of family as well as the many other levels of "community" which exist within the larger church.

In this connection, another key element in the *Order*'s understanding of initiation is the importance of *sponsoring* relationships. In one sense, the entire community "sponsors" new members. But the *Order* also specifies this as a particular ministry in a variety of ways (e.g., sponsors, godparents, parents who "present" their child for initiation, the child's "group of companions" who walk with him/her during the initiation process).

What is crucial for initiation, as opposed to religious education, is that there be relationships in which the child is invited to find embodied, in specific individuals, the Christian way of life that is being offered. Christian initiation is more like an apprenticeship or a mentoring experience than a course of studies; developing a sponsoring relationship is an indispensable element in the process. In the sponsoring relationship a human face is given to the Christian experience, and the universal values of the faith are mediated on a scale and with an individual sensitivity that allow a child to appropriate gospel values in deeply personal ways.

The ideal is for a child's family to be imbued with Christian faith and thus act as primary mediator of these values. But such is not always the case; and, even if it should be, there remains a need for others who will play indispensable parts in the child's gradually expanding "worlds" and in the progressively Christian horizon which is being formed within those worlds.

CELEBRATION, THE HEART OF INITIATION

We mentioned above that initiation involves a community actively engaged in passing on its stories, symbols, values and traditions to the next generation. The *Order* makes clear that this happens in a preeminent way in the context of ritual experience. Crucial to the process of a child's initiation is a set of celebratory experiences that are powerful enough to be *transformative*. The ancient Catholic understanding of sacrament as effecting that which it signifies is at the core of this vision of initiation. Ritual experience does not just summarize or preview the lessons a child is to learn in religious education. Ritual experience itself is catechetical and formative, at a level and with a power that no formal instruction can emulate.

The *Order* refers to the major liturgical experiences involved in the catechumenal journey as the "more intense moments of initiation" (6). Perhaps nowhere else does the *Order* offer a fresher, more significant perspective on how initiation promises children a richer faith formation than could ever be received as part of a training in religious literacy. Ritual is at the heart of initiation, and we will have much to say later on about how this needs to shape parish efforts on behalf of children both unbaptized and already baptized.

The consequences of this insight for parish life are dramatic. Initiation involves a whole new sense of time: It must be the rhythm of the liturgical cycle, not the academic calendar, which governs our efforts to initiate children into the faith.

If communities were truly to awaken to the irreplaceable role played by the worshiping assembly in initiation of children, how might Sunday celebrations differ? Parents who presently want the very best in religious education for their children, but who are content to sit passively through boring liturgies Sunday after Sunday (or, perhaps, who do not even attend church with any regularity) would be forced to re-examine the quality of their own liturgical participation. The same energy we currently witness when a parochial school is threatened with closure might be directed at revitalizing the weekly liturgical celebrations which shape a child's faith every bit as much as Catholic schooling. A parish community that has understood and owned its responsibility to initiate its children will no more tolerate poor liturgical experience than it will put up with religion teachers who inculcate heresy. When initiation becomes a community's priority for its children, impoverished ritual experience is simply intolerable. And, as we know well, the steps required to provide powerful liturgical celebrations as the norm for a community's weekly worship are radical indeed.

These steps are radical because the bottom line for vibrant liturgical celebration is a community of strong, lived faith. At the heart of good liturgy is a community that has undergone real conversion to the gospel of Jesus Christ. Not surprisingly, when the parish agenda for its children is initiation, conversion becomes the heart of the matter, not only for the children but also for the adult community. The *Order* is eloquent and insistent that initiation involves a call to conversion, not only for those being initiated, but also for the community into which they are initiated (1, 4, 6, 9, 252, 253, etc.) Although certainly not its aim, our previous approach to religious education often produced well-informed young people with little or no faith. Having lost the initiatory context and perspective we once had when dealing with our baptized children, we have often unwittingly spawned articulate agnostics and religious illiterates. When initiation is the parish's agenda for its young, such a situation is simply inconceivable, since by definition initiation is a process of coming to faith.

CALLING CHILDREN TO FAITH

We will explore more fully in Chapter Five the nature of conversion integral to the *Order's* initiatory vision. But several corollaries seem important to mention at this point. The first step in the initiation process is a call to faith (initial conversion). The *Order* uses the term evangelization to describe the variety of activities which are encompassed in this first step. Too often, religious education has presumed faith instead of calling children to faith. Initiation of children always begins with the call to conversion, and in fact continues to insist throughout the initiation process that the heart of the matter is a deepening commitment to discipleship. We may still have to be patient for a while in explaining why we look for deep conversion from those who are members of our Catholic communities. But if we do not blink, if we hold firm to the initiatory vision of the *Order*, subsequent generations will look back with puzzlement on a church of the late twentieth century where folks were surprised when real faith and commitment were asked of them.

The *Order* says that the initiation of children requires "a conversion that is personal and somewhat developed, in proportion to their age . . . adapted both to their spiritual progress . . . and to the catechetical instruction they receive" (253). Both conversion and the initiation process of which it is a part are gradual and progressive, extending over many years. Implied in this insight is the necessity of pastoral formation that is accommodated to the readiness of the child.

The enormous strides that modern catechetics has made in integrating the insights of developmental research can be seen in the *Order*'s repeated caution to adapt all ministerial activity (both ritual and catechetical) to the level of the child. The task of indoctrinating a child with all the "right" answers— whether from the *Baltimore Catechism* or the gospel— is simple indeed compared to the complexity of a pastoral formation that must respect individual rhythms of readiness. Religious education that is based on grade levels makes it appear "normal" to connect sacramental celebrations to a particular age or grade. But the *Order*'s vision of initiation presents a much more complex and highly differentiated set of criteria for sacramental initiation.

A parish that commits itself to initiate its children on the basis of conversion and faith-readiness will be in for a very "messy" kind of pastoral care. Flexible structures attuned to discern individual and family readiness will have to replace scope and sequence charts, mass celebrations of sacraments according to grade level, and arbitrary sacramental guidelines that predetermine the age when a child will be "ready." The trade-off for the inevitable messiness of such a system, of course, is that conversion will remain the heart not only of the initiation of children but of parish life at large. We will become more skilled in discernment, more focused and knowledgeable of the ways of God in ordinary human experience, more sensitive to the behavioral correlates of authentic faith at every age and stage of development.

Underneath the question of the child's readiness is the issue of the community's readiness to initiate the child. It is an exercise in responsibility for the community to take the burden of readiness off the child and shoulder it as its own. In assessing whether or not a community is ready to accept this challenge, one must ask such questions as:

—Does the community embrace children as children?

—Do the community's liturgical celebrations immerse children into symbol and story in rich and powerful ways?

—Does the adult community take care to show its children that their daily experiences are a part of the paschal mystery of Christ?

"SUITABLE CATECHESIS"

Nowhere does the *Order of Christian Initiation* state more succinctly its vision of initiation than where it summarizes the four ways in which a community's initiatory ministries offer catechumens "pastoral formation and guidance, aimed at training them in the Christian life" (75). The four parts of this major section in the *Order* touch on the essence of how a parish carries forward the work of initiation.

First, a "suitable catechesis is provided . . . gradual and complete in its coverage, accommodated to the liturgical year, and solidly supported by celebrations of the word. This catechesis leads the catechumens not only to an appropriate acquaintance with dogmas and precepts but also to a profound sense of the mystery of salvation in which they are to participate" (75.1). Each phrase of this key paragraph is worthy of extended commentary and might well fill a separate volume of its own. It is important to note the connection of this vision with the growing trend toward lectionary-based catechesis.

The trend is more than the latest fad. At the heart of the spiritual renewal called for by Vatican II was an appreciation for the power of God's living word proclaimed in the liturgical assembly, mediating the presence of Christ and calling God's people to faith. The Council directed that "the treasures of the Bible are to be opened up more lavishly so that a richer fare may be provided for the faithful at the table of God's word" (SC 51). This mandate was fulfilled in the creation of our present lectionary with its three-year cycle of Sunday readings and its two-year cycle of weekday texts. In his *Apostolic Constitution* promulgating the Roman Missal, Pope Paul VI pointed with pride to the revised lectionary and the hope of the Council that its use would help to reestablish sacred scripture as "a perpetual source of spiritual life, the chief instrument for handing down Christian doctrine, and the center of all theological study." Many observers have commented on the connection between the lectionary's three-year cycle and the *Order*'s indication that a full catechumenate experience may extend over several years (7, 76).

Clearly, a return to scripture offers renewal for the whole church, not just for catechumens. If initiation is meant to happen for all of our children, not just the unbaptized, then the consequences of a catechesis that is lectionary-based are widespread indeed. We will explore those consequences further in Chapter Four. However, one final aspect of this "suitable catechesis" referred to by the *Order* deserves mention before we move on.

The *Order* indicates that the purpose of this catechesis is to lead catechumens to a "profound sense of the mystery of salvation in which they desire to participate." Clearly, initiation of children embraces more than the narrowly conceptualist approach to indoctrination which is reflected when emphasis is placed on memorized answers to questions from the *Baltimore Catechism*. The legitimate role of memorization in a child's learning process is not at issue here. The point of the *Order* is that initiation invites a child into an experience of the mystery of God and results in a growing desire within the child for a deeper participation in that mysterious experience. How far removed this is from a classroom full of bored students! How great is the challenge we face if we take seriously the vision of initiation evoked by this kind of "suitable catechesis"! The language used in this section of the *Order* is charged with affective overtones and reminds us that initiatory catechesis has more to do with seductive, loving relationships than dry notebooks and graded quizzes.

A GRADUAL PROCESS

The second part of number seventy-five of the *Order* is dense with insight into how initiation is carried forward. It is lengthy but worth quoting in its entirety:

> As they become familiar with the Christian way of life and are helped by the example and support of sponsors, godparents, and the entire Christian community, the catechumens learn to turn more readily to God in prayer, to bear witness to the faith, in all things to keep their hopes set on Christ, to follow supernatural

inspiration in their deeds, and to practice love of neighbor, even at the cost of self-renunciation. Thus formed, "the newly converted set out on a spiritual journey. Already sharing through faith in the mystery of Christ's death and resurrection, they pass from the old to a new nature made perfect in Christ. Since this transition brings with it a progressive change of outlook and conduct, it should become manifest by means of its social consequences and it should develop gradually during the period of the catechumenate. Since the Lord in whom they believe is a sign of contradiction, the newly converted often experience divisions and separations, but they also taste the joy that God gives without measure." (75.2)

The essence of this section may be stated in this fashion: Initiation happens through a gradual process of identification with those who are themselves undergoing conversion to the Paschal Mystery of Christ.

Several dynamics interact here, and we need to point out each of them in turn. First, the example and support of those who are already members of the Christian community are "the way into" the Christian experience for one being initiated. Our remarks above about sponsoring are relevant here. A child is initiated more effectively by following a community's way of life than by "learning about" a variety of religious truths. Next, the significant learnings that one gains from the example of believers have to do with vital elements in the conversion process: how to pray, how to give public witness to one's faith, how to put Christ at the center of one's life, how to discern and follow God's will, how to love others even when the price is self-sacrifice. This section of the *Order* makes clear that initiation has to do with assimilating a new value system ("progressive change of outlook and conduct") and that "social consequences" of this transformation must be evident. There is even the sobering reminder of the painful "divisions and separations" which a believer often experiences. In reading this section, one might well think of those engaged in the ministry of initiation as a community doing "conversion therapy" (the phrase is Aidan Kavanagh's) with its young. Chapter Six attempts to give a practical feel for what such a community might look like.

SHARING CHRIST'S MISSION

The third part of section seventy-five of the *Order* describes the importance of ritual experience in the process of initiation. We have already touched on this issue and will return to it in Chapter Three. Part four of number seventy-five speaks of the final way a community helps to initiate into the Christian faith: showing by example how to live a life of apostolic witness. In one sense, this brief section is the key to what initiation is all about. The *Order* portrays the entire process of initiation as a protracted time of formation for Christian mission. The aim of the

Christian life is not simply a self-absorbed enjoyment of the benefits of redemption. Rather, Christ's call to conversion is a call to discipleship, an invitation to followers who would share his mission to proclaim God's reign, and who are ready to do this here and now by a ministry of reconciliation and work for justice in the world.

Taking seriously this dimension of initiation reveals how limited have been our religious education efforts in the past. Nor is this section of the *Order* talking about the "service project" mentality found in some contemporary confirmation programs which claim their inspiration from the *Order*. The frenzied last-minute efforts of youngsters to tally up the required number of hours in order to get the sacramental prize is a trivialization and a travesty of what the *Order* envisions here as integral to the process of initiation. The initiation of children called for here is a process of forming deeply in them a love for the work of the gospel. Caring for the marginalized, political action for justice, readiness to share publicly the reasons for one's faith, a sense of empowerment for mission rooted in baptism, these are characteristics of the "way of life" into which our young are initiated as they gradually walk with a community of believers for whom such a lifestyle has become "second nature."

We see in section seventy-five of the *Order* a powerful summary of the vision of initiation which will be developed in more detail in the chapters which follow. It should be clear by now that the "paradigm shift" which is offered in this vision has dramatic consequences for a parish's establishment of a children's catechumenate, for how a parish initiates its children who are already baptized, and even for the fundamental ways a parish at large goes about the business of being Christian. A church that initiates has conversion as its agenda, community as its context, and discipleship as its goal. Our focus now turns to several of the specific areas which seem most crucial for the effective realization of this vision.

Questions for Group Discussion

1. "A church that initiates has conversion as its agenda, community as its context, and discipleship as its goal."

a. In what ways does your parish live out this ecclesiology in its vision, goals and practices?

b. In what ways does it fall short?

2. "Initiation is the responsibility of the whole community."

a. In what ways can children be more connected to the larger parish community?

b. Are there ways of developing the consciousness of the larger community to their task of initiating the young?

3. On a scale of 1 to 10, how would you assess the liturgical celebrations of your parish from a child's perspective?

Give reasons and specific examples of why you gave that rating. What would you suggest to further enhance the liturgical experience for children and adults?

4. Overall, how would you describe your own parish's readiness to initiate its children?

3. Liturgical Rites

> The church, like a mother, helps the catechumens on their journey by means of suitable liturgical rites, which purify the catechumens little by little and strengthen them with God's blessing. (RCIA 75.3)

Many a "traditionalist" Catholic today crying for a return to the *Baltimore Catechism* would be surprised to learn that the catechism as we know it was a creation of the Protestant Reformation. The question-and-answer format which allowed succinct formulations of doctrinal positions, easily committed to memory, is an innovation of relatively recent date used by the Reformers to spread their view of things among the masses. Quickly copied by the Catholic Counter-Reformation, the idea now appears to the historically short-sighted as the "traditional" Catholic way of doing catechesis. In fact, our tradition offers a far more ancient, far better alternative that is particularly apt with children.

When the Fathers of Vatican II taught that the liturgy is the "source and summit" of the Christian life, they were merely reiterating one of our most venerable insights.

LITURGY, THE SCHOOL OF FAITH

"Ritual catechesis" is one of the newly coined phrases being used by those reflecting on what happens when adults and children experience gradual initiation into the Paschal Mystery through the structures set up in the *Order of Christian Initiation of Adults*. It is not a term used in the *Order*; however, it is a reality constituted in the celebration of the periods and steps of the *Order* and is as old as the church itself.

"Ritual catechesis" names the activity of bringing communal faith to consciousness through participation in and celebration of the rites of the community. For example, a neophyte who has been baptized by immersion reflects back on her experience of removing her shoes, jacket and jewelry before entering the immersion pool at the Easter Vigil and says "I thought I was going to die," then immediately follows with the comment "I did, didn't I? That's what this is about: I died to the old Lynn." A parent signs his child's body with the sign of the cross in the presence of the assembly. The gesture evokes the faith and hope offered to the child as she makes her way through the various passages of life with this church as a support.

Or, take another example of ritual catechesis: children and adults, not yet fully initiated, are graciously dismissed from the assembly each week to be nourished at the table of God's word. During their period of preparation for coming to the fullness of the eucharistic table, they long more and more for that day when they will stay and receive communion. Another way of describing ritual catechesis is to say it is in celebration of the rites that people (children and adults) come to know through experience what they have been told about God, Jesus, and the church.

In some quarters today, there is a wary attitude about ritual catechesis. Is it enough? Does it really happen? What about content? Is this what the church teaches we should be doing? Is this a good form to use with children? Isn't a good textbook enough?

Certainly there is evidence that ritual catechesis has a solid historical tradition in our church. Liturgy has long been regarded as the church's "school of faith," an expression which recognizes the formative impact of ritual celebration on participants. The Lukan community which preserved the Emmaus story was keenly aware of how powerful the liturgy can be in shaping the faith experience of an individual or a community. The thinly veiled liturgical structure of the narrative in chapter 24 of Luke's gospel shows that it is precisely in the experience of the ritual breaking of the bread that the disciples come to know and understand. The story is careful to point out that they had already been told about the resurrection and had dismissed the tale as impossible. It was only in the context of ritual celebration that they were finally able to grasp not just the fact of resurrection but its meaning as well. Other examples of liturgy's formative power abound in the pages of the New Testament, where it is frequently clear that a liturgical context is presupposed in order to understand the teaching of a given passage, or where a text seems to have had a liturgical origin and only later to have found its way into the canon of scripture. For the earliest Christian, there was no question of a distinction that rigidly separated catechesis from celebration. The two were like sides of a single coin.

One can easily trace the history of this linkage of liturgy and catechesis across the centuries of the Christian era. One of the periods in which this linkage was most keenly felt was the fourth century, during which the *disciplina arcani* and the art of mystagogy flourished. The *disciplina arcani* refers to the practice common at that time of not telling prospective converts certain core elements of the Christian faith until after (or better, during) their initiation. The full teaching about eucharist, for example, was felt to be so sacred that it could not be shared with them until the time of their sacramental initiation.

This hesitancy on the part of the community was a result of its conviction that the converts actually were incapable of understanding the church's teachings on eucharist until they had undergone the experience of the ritual celebration. Once they had taken part in the celebration, then and only then could they begin to grasp what the awesome mystery is about.

This practice of the secret gave rise to the development of mystagogical catechesis, which is a particular kind of instruction on the initiation rites just completed. The classic examples of those instructions which have come down to us from Ambrose, Augustine, Cyril of Jerusalem, Chrysostom and others offer a glimpse of a highly developed interaction between ritual experience and catechetical instruction. It is impossible to say that these are instructions about rituals, just as one cannot say that the rituals alone were self-explanatory of the experience. What we observe is a balanced interaction in which converts have been led to a heightened openness and expectancy before the ritual, and then immersed in an incredibly rich sensory experience laden with meaning, which in turn is "unpacked" for them in a series of carefully orchestrated instructions that build on their experience. Ritual experience gives substance to mystagogy. Mystagogy in turn opens up the ritual in a way that allows personal appropriation of its meaning.

After the era of Christianity's rapid expansion, with the corresponding decline in emphasis on adult initiation that was experienced, it is in the growth of monastic communities that we can most easily trace how ritual catechesis continued to flourish in the church's life. What had started quite simply in

Judeo-Christian communities of the first century as a pattern of prayer using psalmody and sacred scripture in the morning and evening was to evolve quickly into the full cycle of the liturgy of the hours. The rise of great monastic communities, first in the deserts of the East and later in the agricultural fields of the West, brought with it the need to school great numbers of semi-barbaric novices in the ways of God. The elaborate choreography of ritual action that grew up around the cycle of the hours was meant to teach the young monks (and their elders as well) the mysteries of God and how one lives successfully according to the divine plan. That the monasteries should have kept ablaze almost single-handedly the richness of Christian faith throughout the so-called Dark Ages is testament to the effectiveness of ritual catechesis.

But it is not just with new converts or monastic communities that the church has used ritual catechesis as its primary means of forming Christians in the faith. Indeed, for the mass of believers from the beginning up into the modern era, it was in the context of liturgical celebration that catechesis normally occurred. There is little written record of how this took place, since it happened so naturally as not even to be noticed. Our richest written legacy, of course, is in the collection of sermons preached during liturgical celebrations, from earliest days—witness the texts that found their way into the books of the New Testament (e.g., 1 Peter)—in unbroken succession into our own time. This vast corpus, which is still used to supply daily readings during the liturgy of the hours, shows how preachers of every generation built upon the liturgical experiences of their hearers to deepen and develop the experience of Christian faith which was being celebrated.

Other evidence, often overlooked, of how the liturgical context was used to form the faith of the masses is to be found in the history of Christian iconography. From earliest centuries, Christians decorated their places of worship with symbols of faith that could be read and grasped by illiterate believers who had only to open their eyes in order to be instructed on the meaning of the mysteries they had gathered to celebrate.

One thinks of the rich symbols in the ancient churches and baptistries of Ravenna, where fifth and sixth century neophytes emerged from the baptismal waters under the glow of golden domes which portrayed the garden of paradise, the new creation, Jesus welcoming Noah from the ark, lands of milk and honey, and more. Led to the eucharistic table for the first time, these new converts could stand in the great apse of San Apollinare in Classe and listen to the prayers of the Roman canon about "the gifts of your servant Abel, the sacrifice of Abraham . . . and the bread and wine offered by your priest Melchisedech," all the while gazing up at the massive transept above the altar from which peered back at them the figures of those same three precursors of

Christian eucharist! The mosaics of ancient Roman basilicas and the frescoed walls of churches large and small, from one end of Christendom to the other, are veritable textbooks of Christian catechetical activity, invariably echoing in the language of iconography the ritual activity over which they presided.

This quick look back over the centuries is meant to remind the reader of the fact that, for most of the Christian era, the primary place of catechetical activity was in the midst of the liturgical assembly, not in classrooms or their equivalent. One came to know what it meant to be Christian, what a Christian believed and how a Christian should act, by participating in the source and summit of our Christian experience, the liturgy. Immersion in the "world" created out of liturgical experience was the normal, ordinary way for adult and child alike to be formed in the faith.

An ancient Latin axiom, still frequently used today, reinforces the primacy of liturgical experience for an authentic appropriation of the Christian faith. *"Lex orandi legem credendi statuit"* (the rule of prayer establishes the rule of faith) is the dictum whose earliest written trace is found in the fifth century work of Prosper of Aquitane, but which was already considered an ancient standard by that time. Basically, this saying insists that in the experience of the church at prayer we have a privileged encounter with Christian faith in its most authentic expression. In times of heresy, theological dispute or questionable practice, the church can discern God's truth in its most pure form if we listen to how the Spirit has taught us to pray. Liturgy, in fact, was formerly called *primary theology* (i.e., a first reflection on our experience of God) while what we popularly call "theology" today was at that time termed *secondary theology*. The point is that in the praying church one can come as close as humanly possible to a direct experience of God. Every subsequent reflection on or teaching about that experience is somehow derivative and must acknowledge its secondary role vis-à-vis liturgical experience.

This does not mean that the place of theological reflection and catechesis is of little importance in the life of the church. It does mean, however, that both theology and catechesis must recognize that liturgy is the Christian's primary formative experience of Christian faith.

AWAKENING THE LONGING FOR GOD

The human sciences too show us the primacy of liturgical experience. Research on moral and religious development of children supports the importance of what we have come to name as ritual catechesis. The work of Jean Piaget on the cognitive development of children from infancy through adolescence has been foundational for a vast array of specialized studies in many areas of developmental research. Work has been done on affective development from the psychological perspective, on cognitive functioning from the

perspective of learning theory, on moral development and on faith development. The literature in
these fields is highly sophisticated and quite articulate. Without pretending to capture the nuance possible in the work of specialists, we can nonetheless
report here on some of their findings which seem
most relevant to our concern with ritual catechesis.

Their research shows that learning is not something which commences in a child at the age of reason or when formal schooling begins. In fact, some of
a child's deepest, most formative learnings take
place in the pre-logical years of early childhood, long
before society's period of formal education. Many of
the most important experiences which, in the words
of Paul Philibert, "landscape the religious imagination of the child"[1] are given to the child during the
early years well before formal catechesis generally
begins. Images of religion—God, heaven, holiness—
are impressed deeply upon the young child in formative encounters with rituals where these realities
are symbolically expressed. Basic experiences of
belonging lay the groundwork for later understand-
ings of community, the people of God, and even salvation described in relational terms. Affective
experience arises first from parental bonds and from
relationships within a child's gradually expanding
horizon of others. That affective bonding is further
developed vis-à-vis a God who is presented as One
who knows and loves us, calls for a response, enters
into relationship with us.

Joseph Gelineau, speaking about the *Directory for Masses with Children* has some important reflections in this regard:

> One is thus directed toward the core of any initiation, which is the education of longing, within a cultural milieu. Nothing will happen if one does not start by awakening the longing for God, the feel for spiritual realities; if one does not provide stages, landings, challenges, which alone can cause the longing to grow; if all of that is not done within a group of believers (culture) which by its symbolic stories (Bible) and its symbolic gesture (rites) imposes a pattern on this longing and gives it meaning.[2]

In the pre-logical child especially but also in early childhood after the onset of logical thought, where more deeply to encounter one's first formative experiences of religion than in the liturgical context? Research has shown that it is through story and symbol, in the affectively charged context of familiar rituals, that the child is impressed most deeply in the ways that are formative of faith. Obviously, it is in the context of the liturgical assembly that the Christian community is best able to provide this for its children. It is the liturgy, whose grammar and syntax are symbol, story and ritual, that best meets the child's readiness to learn at the appropriate level. And, because of the multi-faceted nature of symbol and story in the ritual context, the experience is available to virtually every level of development.

CELEBRATING THE STORY

Another scientific discipline that has contributed greatly to our appreciation for the privileged place of liturgy in faith development is cultural anthropology. The careful observations that have been done on how societies function, how they instill members' identities, how they transmit values and preserve order, all highlight the central role of story and ritual. Cultural anthropology has helped us to understand how our Christian liturgies are part of the universal human phenomenon in which a social group enacts its foundational story within a ritual context. The story is made up of images (i.e., symbolic code) which tell the group the basic truths of existence: Who is God? Who are we? Where do we come from? Where are we going? Why is there suffering and death? What is the origin of good and evil? etc. The ritual re-enactment of the story allows participants to learn its truths, but permits them also to appropriate personal identity ("I am God's child") and to assimilate *meanings* beyond the mere recitation of facts ("the cross means divine love, not just torture").

In order for the formative impact of the ritual to be maximized, several things are essential. Most important, the symbols used in the rite must be richly expressive. If the story is told in muted language, its impact is lessened. If the ritual is full of rich, primal symbols, its power to shape the consciousness of the participants is proportionately increased. A second essential characteristic is that the community performing the ritual be committed to its "success." That means several things: participants must believe in the truth of the story and in the expected outcome of the rite; they must also enter fully into the ritual enactment according to their assigned role. (Some rites call for both silent observers and active participants. When those who should be active become passive, the rite is crippled and its "power" lessened.) Where a ritual is performed with great "earnestness" by every member of the community, i.e., when everyone believes completely in the power of the rite and its truth, and everyone participates fully as expected by the rite, then the formative experience is maximized, especially for children who are uniquely open to its ritual language.

By now the consequences of these insights for ritual catechesis with children should be becoming clearer. We need to realize that our communities' liturgical experiences are the primary way in which catechesis is done for our children, from infancy through early childhood. All of the faith-sharing done by parents in the home should prepare for and flow from the community's liturgical gatherings. The great stories of our faith and the primary symbols used in our liturgies should be the core curriculum around which we build catechetical experiences. The church has already provided the framework needed for initial catechesis in the annual liturgical cycle, in the three year pattern of lectionary texts, and in the symbolic repertoire used as part of our ritual tradition. Initiation, as described in the previous chapter, involves a progressive immersion of the child into the entire range of a community's ritual life. It is unthinkable that a parent would decide not to bring the child to Sunday worship "until he learns to behave" (at age 5? 10? 15?). From infancy onwards, children's place is in the midst of the liturgical assembly.

THE NEW SHAPE OF SUNDAY

This will place a new set of demands on the American parish in terms of creative use both of space and personnel. Imagine a typical Sunday morning assembly where, after the usual greetings of friends and strangers, a gathering song is sung and the presider welcomes those present and gives an introduction to the day's celebration. When the introductory rites are concluded with the opening prayer, everyone is seated and each group of children with their catechist is called forward in turn. Beginning with the three- and four-year-olds, and continuing up to age twelve, each group is given an admonition by the presider, and then the catechist is entrusted with a children's lectionary and instructed to break open God's word for the children. The groups leave in solemn liturgical procession to a separate space nearby where that day's readings (the same ones heard by the adult community) are proclaimed using texts suited to the child's ability to comprehend. The children experience a liturgical ritual, not a class-room exercise. The atmosphere is prayerful; readers proclaim texts introduced and ended with the appropriate liturgical cues; psalms are sung in response; homiletic reflections lead into catechetical experiences which involve the groups at their own level; and the word service concludes with some elements of creedal profession and intercessory prayer. Ritual gesture and generous use of symbol mark the experience: not the weak, contrived symbols so often seen today in children's celebrations (felt cutouts of hands for banners, butterflies, etc.), but the robust, primal symbols of our liturgical tradition (light, water, oil, bread, wine, incense, bows and touch).

On the particular Sunday we are imagining, the gospel text is Jesus' proclamation of the beatitudes ("Blessed are the peacemakers . . ."), a story that invites catechetical use of a variety of symbols from the tradition. The younger children use a simplified version of the sprinkling rite from the Sunday renewal of baptism to learn about the blessed peace that comes from this sacrament of forgiveness. Other groups use the laying of hands on the head, which they will someday experience in the sacrament of penance, to discover how peace is made when we touch one another in healing ways. An older group focuses on the sign of peace which marks every eucharistic celebration, and connects that to the way peace is made at home so that important celebrations are not marred by anger or hurt. In the adult com-

munity, the homilist has spoken of the Jewish proph-
ets who used symbolic gesture as a form of perfor-
mative utterance, and this has been connected to the
contemporary peace movement and the parish's Pax
Christi group, with an additional challenge to recognize which symbols in the eucharistic liturgy qualify
as committing the assembly to building peace in
more proactive ways.

The catechists in the children's groups think of
themselves more as leaders of worship than as teachers. Materials provided by commercial publishers
follow the lead of the liturgical season and the lectionary, not an arbitrary curriculum. Background
material for the leader gives a feel for the liturgical
context, the history of the season, simple exegesis of
the scriptures, and creative use of symbols that fit
with the tradition. Children's materials invite them
to interact with the word proclaimed in light of their
own life experience. They are being shown, from the
beginning, how to hear the scripture as guide and
source of meaning for daily life.

Some of the children have already been fully initiated through the three sacraments of initiation
(baptism, confirmation and eucharist) in infancy.
These return to join the adult assembly for the
eucharistic prayer. Others have been baptized as
infants but still await confirmation and eucharist, or
are catechumens who have yet to receive any of the
sacraments; all of these children remain with their
peer groups until after the adult community has

completed communion. (Everyone learns from the beginning, because it is their experience, that initiation is about becoming a member who partakes of full fellowship at the table.) Religious publishers will have a variety of materials available for use in the home during the week, again at several developmental levels, which will allow further implications of the liturgical faith experience to be explored and assimilated by the family together.

This pattern will be the normal way Sunday is celebrated all year round. Since ritual catechesis is tied to the liturgical cycle, not the academic year, neither children nor adults ever "graduate" and leave behind its challenge to grow in faith. No attempt is made at organizing a systematic curriculum during the early childhood years when the focus of faith-formation is concentrated on the Sunday liturgical experience. In the junior high years, when the developmental readiness for a more logical and systematic exploration of experience begins, more formal study and instruction will start. But in the experientially rich formative years from infancy through early childhood, the emphasis is centered on ritual catechesis.

A mystagogical approach to catechesis puts ancient wisdom at the service of a new era, as children are immersed in the rich symbolic world of the liturgy and then gradually, progressively, invited to unpack the meanings discovered in their experience. Developmental research has shown that each succeeding stage of the child's life requires a reworking of the symbolic content absorbed at previous levels. One of the greatest challenges faced by those who try to lead children along the ways of faith is how best to facilitate that process of reworking previous learnings so that they will be assimilated into the learnings of higher stages rather than rejected as outmoded.

The challenge is most acute in the adolescent stage, of course, where healthy development requires a distancing from what has hitherto been imposed by parents and other authority figures. There, the critical reworking process can easily jettison whatever "truths" seem to have been imposed from without. Where ritual catechesis has been a progressive experience of *personal* meaning for the growing youth, the likelihood of a wholesale rejection of Christian faith is lessened considerably. Information "about" and rules of behavior imposed by authority figures are the first to be rejected in the adolescent search for self-constituting meaning. But rich symbolic experience which, over the years, has become meaningful at each successive developmental stage is likely to endure.

If a parish is able to organize its youth ministry so that the tribal instincts of adolescence find identity constituted in a peer group with ownership of liturgical experience, then another crucial threshold will be successfully navigated. In this volume the focus is not on that particular challenge, but our conviction is that good ritual catechesis leading up to the adolescent crisis will make the task considerably easier and more successful.

By now the perceptive reader will no doubt have a gnawing concern that has reached audible proportions: "All this talk about rich symbolic experience and the power of ritual to shape faith! Have you seen what goes on in my parish on Sunday morning?"

As we did in our opening chapter, we begin with an admission of failure. The dream of a church revitalized through a renewed liturgy is still largely in the pages of Vatican II rather than a lived experience in most parishes. But a radical vision is able to look back at the earliest Christian experience and know the power that we hold in our hands. It is able even to discern in our present experience the signs of a return to liturgical celebrations which can be electrifying in their power to transform. The fact is, communities that have taken seriously the challenge and put their best resources into creating liturgies of beauty, dignity, and faith have witnessed the realization of that dream.

Where communities and those entrusted with liturgical leadership have dared to trust the power of the ritual, dramatic changes have occurred. Deeply embedded in our tradition is a keen sense of the power of symbol. Scholastic theologians used the phrase *ex opere operato* to convey the numinous power of liturgical experience. Earlier centuries had a more lively pneumatological sensitivity and were able to recognize the Spirit hovering over baptismal waters and sacred chrism, as well as bread and wine.

Where contemporary communities rediscover the sacramental principle which is our most deeply Catholic treasure, they discover the key to liturgical experience that is truly radical in its repercussions. Our hope for the realization of this vision is well-founded, because good experience "sells" itself. Once our primal liturgical symbols are trusted enough to be used as lavishly as they are meant, their heightened efficacy is self-evident to all who are part of the experience. In a community that has for years heard baptismal homilies about death-resurrection with Christ (Romans 6), but seen only the trickle of water crease a forehead, try baptism by immersion. *Experience* what baptism means when three times the catechumen is plunged into waters that can literally drown; watch the reaction of the community as the candidate rises out of the water gasping for air; and *then* read Romans 6 at the dripping neophyte ("Are you not aware . . ."). Once the symbols of liturgy are trusted, and presiders again become comfortable with ritual action on a public scale that can reach an entire assembly, the vision will become reality.

The key to ritual catechesis, it is true, is a ritual experience worth talking about, one that has touched and moved a community to the point where they have *felt* something happen. This will also require communities of believers who are invested in what is at stake, again a far cry from the typical parish of today. That is why Chapter Five describes conversion as the crucial issue, not just for children, but also for the adult community in which the ritual catechesis takes place. The radical vision of this book embraces a church of believers, where the Sunday assembly is filled with those who want to be there, are eager to participate, and truly believe that their life and the life of the world hinge on what is about to take place.

Questions for Group Discussion

1. "The core of any initiation . . . is the education of longing."

a. What are the longings of the people (adults and children) who come to Mass on Sunday?

b. How are these longings addressed in your parish celebrations?

c. Are there any longings that are not addressed at the liturgy but are addressed elsewhere in the life of your parish?

d. Are there any longings not addressed anywhere at all? Could they be?

2. From a reading of this chapter:

a. How would you define ritual catechesis?

b. How would you rank the effectiveness of your present liturgical celebrations (their use of symbol, music, liturgy of the word) as catechetically effective?

Notes

1. Paul Philibert, *Catechumenate*, March, 1989, p. 35.
2. Joseph Gelineau, "Reflections: Children and Symbols and Five Years after the Directory for Masses with Children," *The Sacred Play of Children*, ed. Diane Apostolos-Cappadona (Seabury Press: New York, 1983), p. 30.

4. A Suitable Pastoral Formation

> The catechumenate is an extended period dur-
> ing which the candidates are given suitable pas-
> toral formation and guidance, aimed at training
> them in the Christian life. (RCIA 75)

A major premise of the present volume is its asser-
tion that we have been attempting to do religious
education with our children before they have been
adequately initiated. Profound changes are in order,
we believe, if we are to alter our habitual ways of
thinking about and doing religious formation for
the young.

It is the contention of the authors that the reme-
dy to many of our present ills lies in devoting an
extended period of time to the initiation of children
before any attempt is made at formal religious education. Specifically, we believe that, through the
intermediate grades, children should be in a process
of initiation, and only with the advent of junior high

(grades 7 and up) is it appropriate to begin a formal and more systematically structured effort at religious education. The result would be a prolonged catechumenal formation for children in their early years.

In this chapter we wish to explore some of the catechetical dimensions of the "suitable pastoral formation" spoken of in the *Order of Christian Initiation* (75). Our focus here as in the rest of this volume is on children of catechetical age through the completion of intermediate grades.

But a preliminary word also needs to be said about youngsters on either side of this age group. We recognize that a change in the way we deal with some of our children will require corresponding changes in the structures which deal with the rest of our young. Parishes will need to offer parents more support and better resources to improve the quality of religious formation in the home during the earlier years of a child's life.

By the age of five a large part of the child's religious horizon has been formed. There is a tragic lack of resources in most parishes for families with preschool children. Along with re-negotiating our present religious education structures, much more attention needs to be paid to connecting with these parents. Young parents are very often far away from their own parents or older siblings. In many parishes they are strangers. They have questions, issues, needs, and concerns about their own marriages, their role as parents, the moral and religious development of their children. Parishes that provide forums and gatherings for these parents to come together, with or without their children, to talk to each other and to older parents in the parish on how they "did" it when their children were young, as well as what mistakes and successes they had, are taking a major positive step in the direction of community building and creating catechetical environments for these families.

Parents need help learning how to use family rituals and how to talk to their children about God and prayer in ways that will provide a positive basis for future catechesis. A good deal of practical wisdom is available today to help parents expose their children to healthy images of God and to provide them with positive symbolic/imaginative religious content upon which to build for a lifetime. Parishes should provide this help.

At the other end of the age spectrum which concerns us, a parish will also have to revise its ways of religious formation in light of the shifts suggested in this volume. During the junior and senior high years, a parish will begin the process of formal religious education that will continue, hopefully, throughout the adult years as well. Ideally, these efforts would be part of a total youth ministry program that has been developed in integral fashion, embracing service dimensions, prayer/retreat components, peer ministry, ritual celebration, formal instruction and so forth.

THE TABLE OF GOD'S WORD

The specific focus of this volume, however, is on how it is that initiatory catechesis is best done during the early years of childhood. We continue to draw from the *Order of Christian Initiation* as a basic source of inspiration.

In the previous chapter we have shown the important role which strong ritual experience must play in the process of initiation. Within the context of ritual experience, a particular form of catechesis has proven to be of singular value in furthering the goals of initiation. Lectionary-based catechesis, as it is called, seems to be a most "suitable catechesis . . . solidly supported by celebrations of the Word" (75.1) as spoken of in the *Order*. Earlier we discussed how this approach works in general fashion; now we need to take a closer look.

In a parish that has committed itself to initiate its young before it begins formal religious education, there would be no religious education program for youngsters prior to junior high, other than the regular gathering for children's liturgy of the word on every Sunday and holy day. Year round, just as it does with adult catechumens, the community would use the assigned lectionary readings as the focal point for catechesis. As indicated in the previous chapter, children would be dismissed at each eucharist in peer groups and would participate in a liturgy of the word aimed specifically at their developmental level, complete with prayer, proclamation of the word, song, ritual gesture, homily and short catechetical session, and so forth. The catechist/leader of prayer would follow the guidelines of the *Directory for Masses with Children*, making full use of its mandate to adapt the celebration to the children's level of readiness.

A variety of materials are already on the market and more will continue to appear that will assist catechists in using the lectionary-based model appropriately and to maximum advantage. Instead of the present system of twenty-some religious education classes following the academic calendar, children would receive catechesis fifty-two weeks of the year, not as an extra burden of instruction or as a replacement for Sunday liturgy, but as the normal way faith is nourished in community. The lectionary-based method is still in its infancy, but already a certain level of expertise is emerging in materials being published from this perspective. Those who feared that lectionary-based catechesis is nothing more than sharing spontaneous reactions to a gospel text have come to see how richly faith can be nourished at the table of God's word through this method.

There are a number of advantages that are clearly present for the community that adopts this approach. At every grade level, children will be reflecting on texts that their parents are hearing in the adult assembly. The possibilities this opens up for family-centered learning are substantial. Take-home materials for family use during the week can provide rich fare for inter-gencrational sharing. Already there are many adult-oriented materials available which help parents to understand the Sunday scriptures in light of our tradition of doctrinal development and moral training. Further, the fact that catechesis is wedded to liturgical celebration ensures that the experience is always offered in a faith context. The teaching of Vatican II about the presence of Christ in the word proclaimed is important here. Initiation of children aims at introducing them to the Living One present in his word. Lectionary-based catechesis that is integral to a powerful ritual experience ensures that children learn to know Christ as present rather than "learn about" abstract religious truths.

The fact that lectionary-based catechesis unfolds according to the rhythms of the liturgical cycle is another of its assets. It is virtually impossible to divest from a religious education program that follows the academic year all of the cultural baggage which goes along with a scholastic mindset. As everyone knows, we "graduate" from (i.e., leave behind) an academic environment. We move on to "real" life where learnings are practical (and valuable). One reason why religious education has failed so miserably is surely that everyone has "graduated" from a religious education program already. On the other hand, children whose early religious formation is initiatory and uses lectionary-based catechesis all year round receive none of those cultural messages.

Children growing up Catholic learn that every Sunday they gather with the community to celebrate word and sacrament, and that this goes on for a lifetime. Lectionary-based catechesis, like the liturgical cycle, is experienced as a continuing process that instills a love for the word strong enough to last a lifetime!

This form of catechesis also helps to train children from the earliest years in the rhythms of the annual cycle of the liturgy. Over time, children come to know as clearly as the professional liturgist the doctrinal resonances of each liturgical feast and season. They may not yet be able to articulate that knowledge in sophisticated terminology, but they learn that Advent is about messianic hope and expectation, not just "Christmas shopping"; they discover the initiatory character of Lent and the mystagogical nature of the Easter season; they discover that feasts are about mariology and christology and the communion of saints. Their language to describe just how the liturgical cycle "unfolds the whole mystery of Christ" (SC 102) may not be as precise as an answer memorized from a catechism, but they know that truth in their guts, because they have experienced it and celebrated it and explored it in catechesis year after year in powerful ritual form.

A further advantage of lectionary-based catechesis is that the stories of scripture so closely follow a child's most natural way of learning. Educators have described in detail the power of story to reach the imagination of the child, to shape values, stir affections and model behaviors. When a child explores the meaning of our sacred stories week after week and year after year, deep impressions are made which etch indelibly within a child the Christian world-view. The child's world is populated with the heroic qualities of Jesus and our other ancestors in faith, not just Batman and Superman. Answers, pre-logical and mysterious, are given to the problem of evil and to life's tragic dimension, as time and time again the story of the dying and rising of Jesus emerges as the central key to life's meaning. Children never tire of the repetition of a good story, and a constant exposure to lectionary-based catechesis throughout childhood leaves in the child lingering memories of delight and wonder at the marvelous tales of Christian faith which have been discovered and explored in the precious book of God's word.

"But do they get adequate content from this method?" The question would be ludicrous did it not betray such a sadly narrow preoccupation with a conceptualist understanding of faith. James Michael Lee's tome on *The Content of Religious Instruction* shows the broad parameters that are more properly used in discussing "content" (as product, process, cognitive, affective, verbal, nonverbal, unconscious, lifestyle) and should effectively silence those whose ideological blinders leave them with such an impoverished notion of content.[1] Of course lectionary-based catechesis provides adequate content! In fact, the rich content of lectionary-based catechesis can barely begin to be tapped in the two or three times that a child would have heard the full three-year cycle during the course of childhood initiation.

OVERCOMING OBSTACLES

In pointing to the many advantages of adopting a lectionary-based model as the primary form of catechesis for initiation, we are not oblivious to the obstacles which a community also faces. Sad to say, one of the greatest hurdles that must be overcome in implementing this approach is the terribly mundane fact of life called "the Mass schedule." In order to do this kind of word-based formation well and with the care it requires, our venerable tradition of get-them-out-so-we-can-clear-the-parking-lot Masses would have to be abandoned. Now, indeed, we are talking ideas that are radical!

The fact is, the paradigm shift being proposed in this volume inevitably forces the issue of intentional faith vs. cultural Catholicism. If we are going to initiate our children through the sort of robust ritual experience described in the previous chapter, and if a careful lectionary-based catechetical experience is to be a regular part of the children's liturgy of the word, then the shape of the adult experience at the Sunday assembly must also change. Simply put, a parish will have to make a commitment to take more time to celebrate in more leisurely fashion the core

mysteries of faith. For those skeptical about the viability of such a change, one need only point to current experience in many Catholic Afro-American and
Hispanic communities today.

The shift is "of a piece"; that is, ultimately the
entire parish community is being asked to adopt a
more intentional style of being church. The practical
details are not really that complex to work out. In the
adult assembly, in fact, greater vitality can also result
when, instead of a boring homily (so the surveys
describe most Catholics' current experience) more
time is spent during the liturgy of the word in dia-
logue homilies, faith sharing/witness and other
appropriate forms of "breaking open" the richness
and relevancy of the word. Yes, Mass schedules have
to be changed to accommodate the more substantive
experience being suggested. But for those who taste
the benefits of this better way, no further convincing
is necessary.

In an earlier chapter on initiation, we discussed
an important section in the *Order of Christian
Initiation* (75) where a description is given of the
"suitable pastoral formation" which constitutes the
catechumenal style of initiation which the authors
suggest holds the key to a better way of forming our
young in the ways of Christian faith. In preliminary
fashion we explored there the four parts of that section which guide our understanding of how the
church is calling us to a ministry of initiation. In considerable detail we have looked at the *Order*'s vision

of how ritual experience must be formative of faith, and in this chapter we have considered the role of lectionary-based catechesis. Now we want to add a few more thoughts on some implications of the other elements in that section of the *Order*.

THE FULLNESS OF CHRISTIAN LIFE

Initiation requires a process of assimilation in which one is immersed into a milieu and learns, as it were, "from within." Parts two and four of section 75 attempt to evoke something of how and in what areas this occurs. Earlier we pointed to the importance of a "sponsoring" dynamic in accomplishing this goal, whether the "sponsor" be a godparent, a family unit, the entire community, or other parish sub-groups. If the shift toward initiation is to be accomplished successfully, parishes will have to spend time, creative energies and material resources developing a variety of strategies complementary to this end.

In the *Order*, sponsorship is a key ministry. In some respects initiation and conversion take place because of sponsorship, since all faith development happens through personal relationship, which is what sponsors provide. Pastoral staffs seeking structures and methods of enhancing conversion should pay more attention to this. Sponsors are guides. They are friends. They witness to the rest of the community about the faith of the candidate. Children need older children and other adults to walk with them at various times during their initiatory experience: adolescents and young adults who will get involved with individual children in apostolic works; adults who will be companions for children in prayer; hospitality ministers who will welcome them and call them by name. In an age when our children are so often anonymous to adults, parishes would do well to call the community to pay attention to its ongoing sponsoring role. In a sense we were letting ourselves off the hook too easily when our focus on children was limited to religious education alone. An initiation model requires that we devise better ways of immersing our young in the full range of Christian experience. Up until now, it may have appeared that the authors are proposing to place all of our eggs in a single basket, i.e., the Sunday experience. We want to make it clear at this point that the scope of our concern is considerably broader.

If action on behalf of justice is a constitutive part of our faith experience, as recent papal teaching has so strongly emphasized, then we need to provide opportunities for children to be introduced into such experiences. The sight of children marching and picketing with parents on behalf of the Right to Life movement is a striking example of how many communities are already accomplishing this. If doing works of charity and justice is integral to Christian life, then we should not wait until the teen years to introduce this notion as part of a confirmation service project.

In the shift we are proposing, fifty former religious education catechists might be redeployed in this fashion: twenty-five would lead the Sunday liturgy of the word and catechetical sessions, ten would develop political advocacy opportunities in which children could meaningfully participate over the course of a year, ten would coordinate children's involvement in parish direct service activities for the poor and marginalized (and build in reflection components to help make connections to their faith commitment), and five would coordinate events to foster the prayer and devotional life of children beyond the Sunday celebrations.

One of the sad losses after Vatican II has been the rich tapestry of devotion that flourished as such an important part of Catholic identity. Some of those traditions may be inappropriate today or irretrievably lost. But others can be rediscovered in fresh ways, and still others await the creative and innovative efforts of coming generations. What is clear, however, is that initiation of children requires the richness of familiar customs and popular devotions as well as the formality of official ritual.

WHEN TO CELEBRATE THE SACRAMENTS OF INITIATION

Thoughtful readers are probably asking themselves how our initiation model of childhood formation manages to negotiate the complexities of sacramental preparation, age, and sequence. A purist position would certainly be the easiest to adopt from a practical standpoint, and in fact would coincide with what the *Order* already requires for children of catechetical age and adults preparing to be baptized: namely, celebrate all three sacraments of initiation in their proper sequence (baptism-confirmation-eucharist) at a single celebration. The *Order* makes it easy to do this for the unbaptized, since it permits no other option. Many feel we should take the cue from the *Order*'s normative status and follow the same policy for all of our children, whether that involves a return to the ancient custom of giving all three sacraments in infancy (as is still the custom in the churches of the East), or follow the Roman custom of waiting until the age of discretion, and then celebrate all three together.

On theological, liturgical and historical grounds the authors favor a purist approach; but our pastoral sense recognizes that such change will come only slowly and will require strong leadership (presently lacking) from those into whose hands, as part of their ministry of apostolic succession, care for the sacraments of initiation has been entrusted in a special way. In the meanwhile, those who live out their Christian life on the parochial level must wrestle with the realities of our current situation.

The current situation, in fact, is a confused and confusing one. We currently have a variety of policies regarding sacramental age, preparation, and sequence which are clearly at odds with each other both theologically and pastorally. Nowhere is this fact more evident than at the Easter Vigil, when senior high confirmation candidates indoctrinated with a theology of confirmation as sacrament of maturity gasp in disbelief as a nine-year-old is baptized, confirmed and given first eucharist. In one parish, confirmation is celebrated at the time of first eucharist (around grade two) after a relatively brief period of preparation, while in the next parish junior high youths must engage in a mandatory two-year "program" before being given the sacramental "prize."

In sorting out these questions, we would like to distinguish three separate though interrelated issues. The first issue is one's basic understanding of what sacrament is: how it is related to individual and communal faith, how it works, and what its relationship is to life experience. The second issue concerns sacramental preparation: how much or little is appropriate and when, who should do it for/to whom, the role parents should play, and the setting(s) in which it best occurs. The final issue is sacramental age and sequence: when and in what sequence each of the three sacraments of initiation should be celebrated, and where in all of this the sacrament of penance belongs.

Resolution of all these issues will have to await another volume (and probably another generation). To discuss a general understanding of sacrament would surely take us well beyond the focus of this book, although it should be relatively easy to recognize the theological vision from which the authors are operating. Most readers of this volume will have little possibility of changing the current policies under which they live regarding sacramental age and sequence. For those who can effect some change, the authors would strongly urge a purist position regarding sequence (baptism-confirmation-eucharist) and would gladly negotiate on the age issue in light of pastoral realities at the local level. For most of us in the foreseeable future, however, the real issue will be sacramental preparation in light of what will undoubtedly remain for years a confusing praxis regarding age and sequence.

The issue, we believe, is best framed in terms of the vision of initiation being proposed in this book. Once a parish has made a commitment to initiate all of its children according to the vision of the *Order of Christian Initiation*, how might preparation best happen for the sacraments of initiation? Children of catechetical age seeking baptism are easily dealt with since the *Order* spells out in detail the full panoply of their initiation process. More problematic is the case of those children baptized in infancy. Once we have eliminated the traditional structures of religious education in opting for an initiation model, how do Suzie and Johnny get prepared for first eucharist?

Our vision of initiation suggests that immediate sacramental preparation is best done within the context of the domestic church, the family, and not as part of any specific grade or class. Church documents are quick to assert that it is primarily the responsibility of parents to form their children in the ways of faith. However, if we are to do more than just utter admonitions, parishes will have to start providing parents with resources that will help them gain self-confidence and develop skills for the task of preparing children for sacraments. Parishes might also provide opportunities for groups of children and their families to gather for days of prayer or other ritual celebrations in order to allow for an experience of the broader communal implications of sacrament.

In this approach, parents are provided with whatever materials are most appropriate for the age and developmental stage of their child. Some families might be working simultaneously with a five- and eight-year-old, both of whom the parents judge ready for eucharist, while their neighbors are preparing a ten-year-old for penance. Like many other features of the initiation model, catechesis for sacraments will be "messy" because it becomes highly differentiated and adapted to individual needs and conversion. But once we let go of our preoccupation with orderly progression, much greater values will come to the fore, like readiness, discernment, conversion, and so forth.

The practical consequence in the long run will be to re-contextualize sacrament in our Catholic experience, so that we will no longer see it as "prize" for good behavior, nor as routine ritual tied to age/grade/course work. Rather, sacraments will more clearly emerge as the natural way a believer expresses and deepens a commitment to the Christian way of life in the public setting of a community of faith.

Some may object that such a system of placing responsibility for sacramental preparation primarily on parents will penalize the child whose parents are of marginal faith. This is true in one sense, but the child is already penalized by being part of a family where there is only minimal faith. In fact, a more honest, reality-based praxis will prevail in this approach, rather than a continuation of the sham of celebrating first communion with a child when neither the child nor the family participates in Sunday eucharist.

Once again, we see that an initiatory vision is ultimately antithetical to a shallow cultural Catholicism. Or, to put it more positively, when a parish opts to initiate its children, they, their families and the parish at large are inexorably confronted with the gospel call to conversion, committed discipleship, and lived faith. Meaningful participation in communal life, reordered priorities that demand a changed lifestyle, and an experience of liturgical celebrations that connect ritual and everyday life are then inescapable. This, it seems, is the fruit of that "suitable pastoral formation and guidance, aimed at training them in the Christian life" (75) spoken of in the *Order of Christian Initiation*.

Questions for Group Discussion

1. The authors contend that an extended period of time needs to be spent initiating children before any attempt is made at formal religious education.

a. What do you envision as the positive effects on children, families, and parish life if you were to adopt this as a practice in your parish?

b. What do you see as major obstacles to implementing this vision?

2. The following are suggested as components in a model of "suitable pastoral formation":
   —support for families with young children
   —bonding and interaction of children with adults in the parish
   —strong ritual catechesis
   —lectionary-based catechesis
   —sponsoring relationships.
List all of the present programs and structures in your parish that include children and/or families, and describe how they incorporate any or all of these components.

3. In looking back over this chapter, and at your present parish experience,
a. what would you most want to change in that parish experience?

b. what would you most want to keep and develop?

c. how would your budget and staff change if your parish pursued a "suitable pastoral formation" of children?

Note

1. James Michael Lee, *The Content of Religious Instruction* (Birmingham: Religious Education Press, 1985).

5. Conversion that Is Personal and Developed

> The Christian initiation of these children
> requires both a conversion that is personal and
> somewhat developed, in proportion to their age
> and the assistance of the education they need.
> (RCIA 253)

In one of the earliest commentaries on the *Order of Christian Initiation of Adults* to appear after its promulgation, Aidan Kavanagh pointed to the broad implications which the *Order* holds for the church at large:

> Initiation defines simultaneously both the
> Christian and the church, and the definition is
> unsubordinated to any other except the gospel
> itself, no matter from what source other defini-
> tions may originate. This being the case, theo-
> logical discourse, canonical reform, religious
> education, ministerial training programs and
> even the practical day-to-day running of dioce-

ses and parishes will find it impossible not to take the present document (i.e., the RCIA) as their starting point . . .[1]

Skeptics were quick to dismiss such claims, and many today would still find Kavanagh's rhetoric overblown. But those who understand how initiatory rituals function in the formation of any religious group know the truth of those prophetic claims. The rites of initiation tell new members what it means to belong to a particular group; but even more deeply, those rituals remind the group of its core identity and call it to reinvest in the meanings which the rites of initiation celebrate. Kavanagh sees another, deeper reason why this anthropological fact is verified in the *Order*. It is, he states, because in the process of initiation the church focuses in a sustained way on the experience of conversion, conversion to Jesus Christ dying and rising in the endless cycle we call the paschal mystery. And, when we are drawn into the heart of the paschal mystery, we find ourselves, in Kavanagh's words, "at the storm-center of the universe."

CONVERSION, THE CORE CONCERN

This has been verified on a practical level in community after community which has undertaken the implementation of the *Order* and gradually been drawn to recognize that the call to conversion is addressed not just to those undergoing initiation, but to the entire parish community. Full implementation of the *Order* has a way of forcing parishes to confront a whole host of gospel-related issues, not least of which is the way pastoral priorities are ranked in the everyday life of the parish. The insistent call of the Lord to "repent" in order to experience the liberating good news of God's reign keeps dislodging the numbing encrustations of cultural Catholicism that threaten the vitality of every parish community. Where more and more pastoral energies are channeled into fostering a life-changing encounter with the paschal mystery, parish programs, parish structures, eventually even the hearts of parish members give way before the seductive call of a God who longs to enter into covenant relationship with us in the blood of Christ.

The most practical consequence of this gradual process of transformation is that the parish begins to look for, expect, and work toward conversion as the goal of all its efforts. A parish that has embraced this initiatory vision in the other areas of its life comes quickly to recognize that the same forces must prevail in its efforts to care pastorally for its children.

During the revivalistic fervor of the Great Awakening of the last century, Horace Bushnell's *Discourses on Christian Nurture* was able to polarize debate over whether a Christian community should be about the business of educating its children or calling them to personal conversion. It is a debate that has resurfaced in various forms among religious educators for more than a century. The inclusive vision of initiation which is found in the *Order* effectively overcomes such dichotomous thinking once and for all. The responsibility of an initiating community is broadly educative and formative, but every pastoral effort is at the service of conversion, the heart of the matter. For a community that wishes to initiate its young into an experience of Jesus Christ dying and rising, there is only one option: to make conversion the primary, irreplaceable, unrelenting core of all its concerns for the next generation. Training for religious literacy becomes a valuable but clearly secondary handmaiden in the pastoral care extended to the young.

The fact that the *Order* includes the initiation of children within its circle of concern means that its vision of conversion holds both for adults and for children. It is true that accommodation of the adult understanding must be made in this area, as in other areas. But it is important to underline the fact that the *Order*'s call for conversion is directed as much to the young as to their elders.

What then is the *Order*'s understanding of conversion, and how are we to apply this to the initiation of children in a parish setting? These are the concerns that will occupy us for the remainder of this chapter.

HELPING CHILDREN GROW IN RELATIONSHIP WITH GOD

The *Order*, in speaking of conversion, often uses the language of covenant to describe what occurs. This terminology, borrowed from the scriptures, is a

kind of "code" language used to indicate that conversion is a relational dynamic. Conversion is an
interpersonal phenomenon. It has to do with the
establishment of a network of saving relationships.
Initiation calls a child into a series of relationships
which are experienced as redemptive. At root, the
core experience of conversion involves a vital relationship with God. Conversion for a child is a dis-
covery that God has initiated a love relationship with
him or her on a very personal level. The *Order* insists
further that it is in the person of Jesus that one most
fully encounters the face of a God who invites into
deep, personal relationship. Of course, that relationship is not with God alone, but with God incarnate in
the body of Christ, the church.

A priority in determining content and processes
for an initiation of children that has conversion as its
agenda is to do the things that will facilitate the
growth of a child's experience and relationship with
God. Most of our current religious education programs and texts pay little attention to this endeavor.
One cannot assume, because children are in a religion class, that this relationship has been developed.
"God talk" is not ordinary in the lives of our children
today. However, children at this age level are able to
narrate their experience of God, if asked and listened
to, and they are able to understand others' experience of God.

Most children in initiation processes are at what
James Fowler terms the mythic-literal stage. This is

the stage, he says, in which one "begins to take on for oneself the stories, beliefs and observances that symbolize belonging to his or her community."[2] In this stage the meaning is both carried and "trapped" in the narrative. Conversion processes need to provide time for children to tell their stories of what God is like for them. Sessions also need to be developed where children are able to listen to and hear and see images and stories of God from their peers and significant adults.

Care and attention need to be given to what images children prefer in the telling of their stories, because images of God are more fundamental to one's faith life than ideas of God. In *The Grammar of Assent*, John Henry Newman states that "belief in God originates in our imagination."[3] An initiatory catechesis on God includes offering other images to children and presenting images from both the Hebrew scriptures and the New Testament stories of Jesus about God for the child to pursue.

The most significant component in deepening our human relationships and our relationship with God is communication. In the religious/spiritual sphere we call this prayer. Much time and attention have been given in the past to having children learn prayers. Too little time has been spent teaching children to pray or providing varieties of prayer experiences for children. The *Order of Christian Initiation* emphasizes the importance of discerning the conversion of persons through their growth in prayer. One of the elements to develop in today's religious formation of children is the area of prayer. There are structured ways to incorporate this into parish life: Family retreat days, time set aside for quiet reflection with children, individual meetings with children to talk about prayer, and so forth. The book *Please Understand Me* has a chapter on children and temperament which would help a catechist or pastoral minister identify with the child and help him or her develop nourishing prayer styles.[4] This area of companioning a child in his/her prayer life is probably one of the most neglected in our present-day process of religious education and one of the most important in conversion.

Another aspect of the biblical notion of covenant is also part of the *Order*'s understanding of conversion: From the human side, any response to God's call must be a free one. In the face of the divine initiative, a person must respond freely and knowingly, or the relationship is something other than authentic conversion. We will have more to say below about how a community must strive to free a child's religious experience from coercive elements which might compromise full freedom.

JESUS AT THE CENTER

A second major element in the *Order*'s understanding of conversion is its emphasis on Christ being at the center of one's faith experience. In our tradition, the person of Jesus Christ must stand at the heart of the conversion experience. If anything or anyone else occupies that position, one's conversion is to that extent faulty or limited. A ministry of initiation with the young must constantly strive to put the story of Jesus before the child in a way that will facilitate this loving embrace. Depending on the age of the child, different images of Jesus may be more or less effective in accomplishing this. Pictures of Jesus the Good Shepherd holding the little lamb may have considerably more appeal to a six-year-old than to a twelve-year-old. Similarly, tales of Jesus confronting the power structure of his day will probably inspire a young adolescent much more readily than they will a child in kindergarten. Sensitivity to the ultimate aim of such stories will ensure that a child's conversion is nourished by introduction to Jesus Christ in ways that are attractive and inviting.

The most significant structure of a catechesis on Jesus has already been explained, that is, lectionary-based catechesis. Here we want to reiterate that one of the major goals of that form of catechesis is to proclaim and present the person and message of Jesus. It is also important to note that an important aspect of discerning children's and adults' conversion is their level of ethical-moral behavior. In the normal course of events children do not ask the question, "Do I want to be good?" Their real question is, "Who do I want to be good like?"

In their presentation of Jesus, catechists and homilists need to bear in mind that children will be attracted to Jesus if he is presented from a very human perspective. He had friends and enemies. He was nice and he got angry. He ate and he fasted. Basically, what we hold out to children is a model. For children to identify with it and begin or continue a conversion to Jesus as Lord, the model must be tenable. Otherwise, children listen and feel shame: "I could never be like that." Another factor to be continually stressed is that it is because of Jesus' prayer relationship with God that he had power, courage, clarity, etc.

IN THE MIDST OF COMMUNITY

The third element and one about which the *Order* is most insistent is its communal nature. Since this aspect of initiation is dealt with at considerable length elsewhere in this volume, we need not say a great deal here. What is important to note is the *Order's* balance in this area. Just as a child is led into a uniquely personal relationship with God, so too must there be a public dimension to the child's faith experience. Conversion, in our tradition, is more than a "Jesus and me" experience. It has an essentially ecclesial aspect to it. A child comes to faith, comes to know God, in the midst of community which itself becomes a revelation of divine presence. Pastoral efforts to involve a child and the child's family in a network of parish relationships are not peripheral to our "conversion therapy." They are at the heart of it.

Could it be that so often conversion does not

happen with our children because we focus solely on the relationship of the child to a catechist and peers? In our present praxis we see concrete examples of children who are brought to first eucharist with less than a minimal relationship to the worshiping community. There are also children who have shared faith only with children their own age. Certainly children can learn in this way and can develop faith. However, in today's world, where religion and faith have so often been excessively privatized, the transformation of lives and communities that results from conversion requires a broader sharing of faith within the church community and a deeper one within the family unit.

James Fowler makes a distinction between development and conversion which might well be applied here to show the importance of the kind of involvement with the Christian community that is essential for families and children if conversion is to be our agenda. For Fowler, development is the kind of transformation that takes place when there are transitions from one faith stage to the next. He states, "A structural change represents a qualitative transformation in the ways faith appropriates the contents of religious or ideological traditions."[5] In the religious education of children, careful attention has been given to the developmental aspects of faithing in content and method. We have age-appropriate materials; we are careful to present what can be appropriated at a given level. What has been given less attention, except in describing its symptoms, is the force of other competing stories, people, communities, and values which have "faithed" (in the broadest sense of that word) our children. For example, the media and advertising—whether they or we are aware of it or not—operate out of a conversion model.

Fowler describes conversion in this way: "Conversion is a significant recentering of one's previous conscious or unconscious images of value and power and the conscious adoption of a new set of master stories in the commitment to reshape one's life in a new community of interpretation and action."[6] Few could deny either the impact of the media's handing on of master stories and images of value and power or the reality that communications media have replaced the church as the legitimator of behavior.

A significant factor often overlooked in our assessment of the impact, particularly, of television is that it is such a universal equalizer. Television's images, stories, values and signs of transcendence are presented to young, old, black, white, rich and poor alike. These are supported by a pervasive communal ethos, and they take root very early in a child's life. Children carry all of this as part of the fundamental content and context of their lives, yet so often we treat it as peripheral to our efforts at Christian initiation.

The authors believe that it is essential to pay more attention to "the competition," as it were, and to be as intentional about developing structures for conversion as we have been about catechesis which respects developmental readiness. If our efforts with children are to result in a significant recentering of their images of value and power (i.e., away from the seductive lure of the mass media's world view and toward the gospel's), then we must offer a set of master stories that will motivate them to live a committed life within the Christian community.

The vision of the *Order of Christian Initiation* assumes the existence of a community strong enough to compete with a society that offers slick advertising, pop idols and instantaneous gratification. Helping our children become integral members of such a community is the work of Christian initiation. It is not just a matter of casual networking or learning to be nice to each other for the sake of good fellowship. It is a matter of conversion. It is a process, as Fowler describes it, with three movements which might be paraphrased thus:

1. I experience or take part in a community event powerful enough to make my previous images start to disintegrate. They become strange and distant. I am no longer at ease with what I do or how I do it.

2. I begin to respond to other images/stories or values that are presented to me, and I take on new images of God, neighbor, and self.

3. I start to act out of these images within a new community of meaning.

Structures of family-centered or family-cluster catechesis are ideally suited to produce this kind of conversion. One young single mother, recently returned to the church, who had participated in a year-long faith sharing family group recounted her story:

> When I first started in this group I noticed that the children very often interrupted the parents. I found that annoying. I also noticed that the parents paid attention to them. My annoyance grew, and then I remembered that my own parents never paid much attention to me when I was a child, and that I continue to brush aside my own children. When we did the session on images of God I saw and felt how distant mine was and my children's and how different from some of the others. There seemed to be a correlation in warm close experiences of God with the families who paid attention to each other. I started to pay more attention to my children. I am a better parent today—more Christian because of this group. And God and I have a much better relationship.

Consider also the story of the fifth grade boy who, after a few months in a family cluster precatechumenate, was asked what he thought he would gain from becoming part of this community. "Well, I think I will learn how not to be a sore loser. I want to be like Brett (an older boy in the group). He doesn't 'lose it' like I do and I think he learned it here."

Initiation and conversion take place in the midst

of a believing community which is inter-generational. We are accustomed to focus our questions
about conversion on the children. "How do we know
they are ready? How much should they know?"
Instead, parishes serious about initiation need to
look at the community and its structures for catechesis. Is the community's faith strong, vital and
attractive to the children? Are its structures family-
centered and inter-generational? Is its catechesis
filled with images and symbols robust enough to
compete with those of the mass media? If the
answers to these questions are "yes," then children
will be invited into an experience of conversion and
initiation that is truly communal in scope.

A Sacramental Experience

The next element of the *Order*'s vision of conversion which we would like to point out is that conversion is a fundamentally sacramental experience. This
means both that the experience is not a purely interi-
or one, i.e., it must be externalized or "sacramental-
ized," and that the process of conversion is carried
forward in and by our liturgical rituals. Sacramental
celebration is integral to a child's conversion and is
required for a fully authentic experience of faith. In
the American culture there is a prevailing understanding of conversion as a hidden, inner awakening, a moment of graced consciousness within a
person that may or may not find external expression.
Our church's decision to structure the whole initia-

tion process as a public, ritualized process constitutes a clear rejection of the American view.

We insist that sacramentalizing conversion in liturgical ritual is a necessary component of a child's full religious experience. For children in the catechumenal process, there are a variety of ritual forms readily available from the *Order* to accomplish this. For our children baptized in infancy, parishes need to be even more creative as they attempt to initiate by means of rituals marking ongoing conversion. Celebrations of first penance might seem to be perfect opportunities for this to happen. Sadly, that has not been the real experience of most children in their approach to this sacrament. Perhaps as parishes accomplish the shift to initiation for all children, celebrations of first penance as well as a variety of other rituals will be "rediscovered" in their potential to sacramentalize a child's conversion experience. The chapter on ritual catechesis in this volume may offer valuable help in this regard.

In describing conversion, the *Order* borrows yet another scriptural image—the spiritual journey—to describe how the process of coming to faith operates. Many Christian denominations in our society strongly emphasize conversion as an event rather than a process. Some even insist on one's ability to name the specific moment when one surrendered to Jesus as Lord. The *Order* clearly rejects such a rigid view of conversion and sees it instead as a growing and living phenomenon. Insistence on accommodation to a child's level of development appears throughout the *Order* and is further evidence of an understanding of conversion in dynamic terms. Pastoral ministers can be impatient with children no less than with themselves and can easily yield to the temptation to rush a process that requires slow, gradual growth. In such circumstances, the result is always to elicit conformity rather than conversion from a child.

The notion of spiritual journey reminds us that there are rhythms and stages in the conversion process. Sometimes moments of regression and failure are the necessary raw material if a child is to come to know forgiveness and grace as part of the conversion experience. Our present praxis of hoarding children to sacraments at a specific age or grade sabotages this aspect of conversion.

A CHANGE IN OUTLOOK AND BEHAVIOR

The final aspect of conversion we would like to mention as part of the *Order's* vision is the balanced, holistic approach which it takes. The human sciences remind us that a child is a unity whose growth and development go forward on many levels and embrace cognitive, affective, and behavioral dimensions. The *Order* respects this approach in recognizing that conversion must operate on many levels and in every area of a child's life. Sensitive ministry to a child's conversion experience requires that pastoral care be nuanced and multifaceted. For too long religious education has been lopsidedly preoccupied with the cognitive. Initiation demands that we give equal time to the affective and behavioral.

A child's conversion involves "falling in love" with God and with God's people. It means a progressive "change of outlook and conduct" (75.2). It means training in action for justice as well as coming to love the quiet of prayer. Conversion, as the *Order* envisions it, lies at the heart of the process of initiation into a faith community.

Given this understanding of what conversion is and how it functions in an initiatory context, it remains now to spell out further implications of this vision for a parish's ministry to its children. One of the most important things to remember regarding conversion in children is that this notion is always a relative one. That is to say, authentic conversion is always defined in terms of the appropriate developmental capacities of the child. The progressive change experienced by a child as part of the developmental process is intertwined with, but not coextensive with, the change we describe in theological terms as conversion. The interrelationships are subtle, and a nuanced understanding of their respective integrities is crucial to effective pastoral care.

Developmental readiness is often the stage, the necessary foundation, for a decisive breakthrough to a new level of spiritual awareness. But there is a difference, for example, between a growing child's newfound capacity to understand the moral implications of a given situation and the personal decision which is then made on the basis of that understanding. Sometimes the decision, despite a child's knowledge of what is "best," will be made on the basis of self-interest rather than perceived value. When such occurs, the call to conversion has not been heeded, even though developmentally speaking the child may have made a cognitive breakthrough to a higher level of moral understanding.

Much of childhood growth has to do with imitative behavior and personal appropriation of values and attitudes lived by parents and other significant figures in a child's world. For this reason, it seems legitimate to understand this process of internalization as a kind of "primary conversion," analogous to—but still different from—the full adult experience of conversion. The child's drive to please adults and to be accepted by these seemingly omnipotent figures shapes in a foundational way the basic world view and value system that will remain throughout a lifetime.

Parish communities that help adults to be more intentional about their own faith development are contributing in a substantial way to the conversion process of the young. Where parents have the opportunity to come together for faith sharing and other experiences that further their own continuing conversion, they become more eloquent advocates of the Christian way. Within the confines of the domestic church, they exercise the ministry of evangelization as they live lives that are more explicitly Christian, thus better promoting the "primary conversion" of their children. The more thoroughly permeated is a parish's vision with the centrality of conversion for authentic Christian life, the more effectively will parents and others evangelize the young into the initial faith and conversion of which the *Order* speaks. In the religious sphere as in other areas, the more explicit and intentional are the adult community's efforts to pass on to the young its foundational values and experiences, the more likely is such reinforcement to succeed.

One of the most delicate issues faced by those concerned with conversion in the lives of children is how to ensure that the scope of personal freedom is progressively enlarged as the child grows. We have indicated above the importance of imitative behavior in the child's "primary conversion," as the fundamentals of the Christian experience are assimilated long before the child is capable of free choice based on reflective awareness. Yet, we have also stressed that conversion is a free response to the divine call to enter into relationship. Throughout childhood, the young are vulnerable to countless coercive and manipulative possibilities at the hands of adults. In the area of deeply held religious convictions, the temptation is all the more acute for adults to abuse their position vis-à-vis the growing child by exercising a subtle but inappropriate control.

In the days of the *Baltimore Catechism*, but still lingering in the mindset of many contemporary efforts at religious education, *de facto* value was placed on correctly learning certain information and behaving in approved ways. Religious formation so understood is quickly reduced to getting the "right" answers and winning approval through external compliance. But such an approach neglects the child's need to question and the quest for personal meaning which are as essential for the child as for the adult. The *Order* insists—for the child as for the adult—that catechesis and pastoral care constantly reinforce the importance of inviting rather than indoctrinating into faith.

It should be fairly clear that the educational enterprise in our society, given its obsession with testing, scoring, grading, passing/failing, and meeting learning objectives, carries considerable cultural baggage which is antithetical to this spirit of freedom. If the spiritual formation efforts of a community are to escape the assumptions and conditioned behaviors of society's educational system, then initiation must have a quite different look and feel than traditional religious education.

In initiation, children are invited into a relationship with the God of Jesus where what is sought above all is the free surrender of a loving heart. In a community that has grasped this insight, readiness for first eucharist will be judged by quite different standards than the knowledge of what is in the book, or how well prayers have been memorized. (On the other hand, the child who has heard that invitation to the table as a sign of God's limitless love will have probably devoured eagerly the content that is "in the book" and will be quite eloquent in the language of prayer.)

For many it will be frightening and difficult to let go of some of the educational trappings which have marked our efforts to share faith with our young. The risk involved in embracing the initiatory praxis suggested here must seem terribly high. But when we remember the admission of failure which premised our discussion in the opening pages of this volume, it may appear that we do not stand to lose very much after all. In fact, we stand to gain the pearl of great price if we are able to recover conversion as the central axis of our efforts with children.

The battle is not, in the final analysis, for the mind of a child. It is for the child's heart or being. We have seen too many generations of agnostics who are religious literates. We have suffered too many products of Catholic schools whose faith life is reduced to a legalistic Sunday observance. We have been smothered too long under the oppressive blanket of conformity on which cultural Catholicism feeds like a cancer.

Something new is needed, new and better. What better and what more new than to return to the roots of our Christian calling by placing conversion once again at the center of all our efforts? When that is done, we will abide with the One who says, "See, I make all things new."

Questions for Group Discussion

1. The image of conversion in this chapter is "falling in love."

a. What are experiences of conversion you have had or witnessed in other people?

b. Do they fit this image or can you add other images to the understanding?

2. How do your present parish sacramental preparation sessions and guidelines respect and promote the element of conversion? Use the following statements as a spin-off for discussion:

—We respect the freedom of children and families.

—We present the person and message of Christ in ways that proclaim to children both catechetically and liturgically that Christ is the center of our belief.

—We are intentional about children sharing faith with and experiencing the witness of faithful adult models in a variety of ways.

—We support the nurture and development of the spiritual life of our families and children.

3. How does your present experience work against the goal of conversion?

4. If your parish took conversion as its primary agenda (both initial conversion and ongoing conversion) what would have to change?

Notes

1. Aidan Kavanagh, *The Shape of Baptism: The Rite of Christian Initiation* (New York: Pueblo, 1978), p. 145.
2. James W. Fowler, *Stages of Faith* (San Francisco: Harper and Row, 1981), p. 149.
3. John Henry Newman, *The Grammar of Assent* (New York: Doubleday Company, 1955), p. 106.
4. David Kiersey and Marilyn Bates, *Please Understand Me* (Gnosology Books, 1984).
5. Fowler, pp. 275-76.
6. Fowler, pp. 282-83.

6. Within the Community of the Faithful

> The initiation of catechumens is a gradual process that takes place within the community of the faithful. (RCIA 4)

In the preceding pages we have articulated a vision of how parishes might better initiate children into the Christian experience. Both theoretical and pastoral concerns have been treated, but we have not yet had the opportunity to put together all of the pieces of the vision in a single place. In this chapter we propose to describe the shape of parish life in a community which has implemented the ideals set forth above.

It should be clear to the reader by now how important is the statement of the *Order of Christian Initiation* that initiation always takes place "within the community of the faithful" (4). To initiate a child is to make him or her a member of a community, to instill a sense of belonging and personal identity that are defined in reference to a definite community of persons.

THE COMMUNITY OF THE FAMILY

We have seen, however, how complex and slippery a notion "community" can be. In fact, in the process of Christian initiation, a child is actually being incorporated into a series of overlapping groups which constitute the "world" of childhood. The image of a series of concentric circles may be helpful as we envision the child's emerging self, reaching out over the years into an expanding progression of communities. The child's core experience of community, of course, is the family, both on a human developmental level and in religious terms. Since the Second Vatican Council there has been a growing body of literature developing the ancient notion of the family as "domestic church." Popes, bishops, theologians and pastoral ministers have begun to unpack the implications of this insight in ways that are extremely relevant to the issues of this book. This is not the place to repeat those insights, but we wish to underscore in the strongest terms possible how crucial is the core faith community of the family in the process of Christian initiation of children. We wish to make our own the words of Vatican II's *Declaration on Christian Education* that the parents' role in forming a child's life of faith "is so decisive that scarcely anything can compensate for their failure in it" (3).

More positively, we wish to emphasize that even as the growing child moves into successively new circles of community, the family continues to play a decisive role in the way that the values and experiences of those new communities are mediated. As the child's horizons expand to embrace the new communities of play group, school, sport and recreational activities, the family still exercises enormous influence on how the values of those groups are interpreted and judged by the child. Attempts to shield a child from all of the forces in our culture which are unchristian would only produce a child ill-equipped for life in the world.

Parents are forced to make countless decisions on a daily basis about how much of the mass media's propaganda on behalf of consumerism, materialism and so forth they are willing to let their child be exposed to. But the parents' Christian faith can still remain a primary interpretive framework inviting the child to reflect on which of those alluring images are healthy and consistent with Christian values, and which are flawed or even immoral.

Parents also have countless opportunities to enter into the various communities which influence their child and attempt to make them more responsive to Christian values. At PTA meetings where human sexuality curricula are discussed, at sports leagues where scheduling of games on Sunday morning is being considered, in neighborhood association meetings where the drug issue is debated, parents can be agents of evangelization by their advocacy for ways of living that will support Christian family values. At best, however, any family must face the fact that in our secular, pluralistic society the values of the Christian home will always have to compete with other communities whose contrary values are powerfully attractive.

THE COMMUNITY OF THE PARISH

This fact heightens the importance of a broader community than the family where the child can experience a Christian way of life that is equally attractive and also powerfully appealing. The Notre Dame Study of Parish Life has given empirical verification of what most of us already knew—the American parish remains the ecclesial structure which best promises to be that kind of initiatory community. It is the parish community which offers our best hope of providing the milieu in which Christian initiation of children will be supported and enhanced.

In the opening pages of this volume, we recalled how effectively ethnic parishes of another era initiated the young into their Catholic world. We certainly do not wish to suggest that it is possible, or even desirable, to return to that sort of closed cultural community where the church once met a variety of social, recreation, educational and other needs that are nowadays provided by other specialized agencies. The American parish will remain one institution

among many that offers to meet a family's specialized range of needs. But this does not mean that
parish communities are condemned to be unimpor-
tant and only peripheral to people's lives. On the
contrary, it is our contention that parishes are called
to be among the most vital communities in our social
mix. They must be communities with a strong, distinctive identity.

If a parish is to be an effective force in the
Christian initiation of children, it must offer the sort
of experiences described earlier in this book, and it
must do so as a community where belonging and
having a sharply defined Catholic identity are
strongly held values. A parish, in order to be effective in the task of Christian initiation, must have its
own "spirit," its unique identity that sets it off from
others and constitutes the specialness that is savored
by its members.

What we are calling for here is that each parish
should be clear about its own special place amidst all
of the other communities which try to lay claim on
the allegiance of its members. A parish needs to be
specific about its Christian mission; it needs to have
its stories and traditions that everyone knows and
loves; it needs those special social occasions that
allow members to celebrate their identity and
belonging; it needs a set of hopes and dreams that
generates excitement for a shared future. Where such
a parish exists, the task of Christian initiation of children is made substantially easier. Where the core

group of parishioners can generate that kind of vision and organize structures which enable that sort of community life, then initiation of children becomes a very manageable task.

Such a community does not require heroic levels of involvement from its members. In fact, if it wishes to remain healthy, such a parish will probably take steps to ensure that intramural involvements do not consume the bulk of parishioners' energies. Rather, there will be limited ways of involvement open to the broadest possible range of members. Each person will connect with those parts of the parish's life where he/she is most needed or most nourished, and no one will feel they have to do it all. But the overall result will be a community of vitality, diversity and living faith. It will be a parish where the fundamentals of Christian living (community, message, service, and liturgy) are available and flourish. It will be a parish into which children are initiated joyfully—a parish not entirely unlike the community of St. Lena. . . .

A MODEL PARISH

It is Ash Wednesday in the Parish of St. Lena. Tonight fourteen members from the parish's Returning Catholic Group will enter the final stage of their journey back to the church by being formally enrolled in the Order of Penitents. Ministry to alienated and inactive Catholics has flourished at St. Lena's, and the team of sponsors, outreach ministers, and others who work in that area is nearly as large as the RCIA team. On "scrutiny" Sundays, the penitents will ask for and receive special prayers from the assembly, similar to the scrutinies for the elect but adapted to their own situation. They will be formally reconciled at one of several communal penance celebrations held during the week before Holy Thursday, in time to share communion once more at the Mass of the Lord's Supper.

Those communal penance services have taken on great importance in the life of the community, since a variety of groups use the occasion to celebrate the sacrament of reconciliation. Youngsters of various ages make their first penance at these times. Formation for the sacrament with younger children is done by parents in the home, although peer group experiences for the older children have been developed and have become important steps in the process. Since young people have been encouraged to approach the sacrament only when they truly experience the need for reconciliation, most of those who celebrate first penance now are in the years of adolescence and young adulthood. It has been discovered that much of the language that once was used in confirmation preparation about making a personal, more mature commitment fits even better as part of the preparation for this sacrament.

The strong youth program that St. Lena's developed several years ago uses the catechumenal model in all aspects of its ministry, and the track for those preparing for first penance has become one of the most substantial segments of the program. In many ways it reflects what is happening with the adults who are in the Order of Penitents, with components that involve spiritual direction, sponsoring relationships, penitential service activities, and so forth. At tonight's Ash Wednesday celebration, there will be specific recognition not only of the returning Catholics, but also of the candidates for first penance.

St. Lena's learned long ago the wisdom of cancelling all of its regular programs and committee meetings during the season of Lent. The parish takes seriously this time of retreat which prepares for the Paschal Triduum. Before anyone comes forward to receive ashes in the form of the cross, time is given for each person to make specific their intentions regarding penitential discipline. Each household has already received in the mail a list of options provided by the parish for experiences of prayer and service, but the major focus on Ash Wednesday is on helping every person come to a decision about how best to prepare for the renewal of baptismal promises that will be asked at Easter. Children here cannot miss the powerful message of Lent. The experience of so many adults taking seriously this call to conversion is an eloquent reminder in the children's eyes that they too must be about the business of conversion during the Lenten season.

The most important symbols of the Lenten sea-

son, however, are not crosses or ashes. Those catechumens and candidates who have been part of the
catechumenal process for long months and years and
now, finally, are to be elected for full initiation are
themselves the powerful, living symbols of the deepest meaning of the season. In the eyes of the children
the elect seem mysterious, almost magical figures,
even though many of them have become familiar to
the children from months of having seen them at
Mass or as they pass through the halls at the end of
the children's liturgy of the word.

On the first Sunday of Lent, the children are all
called back early from their liturgy of the word
groups to listen to special testimony about what God
has done in the lives of these specially chosen ones.
There are a number of children and adolescents who
are also elected. The younger children do not understand all of what is said by the sponsors and others
who come forward to speak. But the charged atmosphere of the room and the rapt attention of the
adults convinces the youngsters that these people
who are being elected are, indeed, specially chosen
ones. And, when they see the community erupt in
applause as the book of the elect is signed, indelible
memories are being etched in youthful imaginations.

In the following weeks, the children watch these
same sisters and brothers, adults and children, come
forward for special prayers, and they feel their
spines tingle at the haunting tones of the scrutiny
litanies. The children become convinced that there is

an awesome presence in the lives of these special people. One young boy remembers his grandfather telling of the spooky feeling of Lent during his own childhood, when all of the statues were covered in purple cloth. But, surely, nothing can match the sense of mystery that builds each week as the prayers of exorcism over the elect make them become charged symbols of God's power to purify and transform. One child broke down in tears several years ago at the Easter Vigil, when she saw the priest push one of the elect under the water in the big baptismal pool. "I thought he was going to drown her," she sobbed to her mother.

Symbols of death. Symbols of resurrection. Childhood memories and images, buried deep in consciousness, shape a faith in the Christian experience. In St. Lena's parish, there aren't very many lesson plans for the children about the meaning of Lent. But the children of St. Lena's *understand* because they *experience*. In fact, during the fifty days of mystagogia, most of the focus with children (as with adults) is on helping them to understand what they have experienced in the vivid sights and sounds, feels and smells of Lent-Easter.

At the Easter Vigil, of course, the parish's initiatory fervor reaches climactic proportions. Outsiders still laugh about the parish's three-hour vigil service, but they fail to understand the relaxed atmosphere that permits folks to go out and "take a break" when they need to (though, surprisingly, most remain for the whole service and say it "flew" by). Needless to say, the symbols used at the vigil are rich and full: light, word, water, oil, bread, wine, a welcoming community. Afterwards, one of the neophytes was once heard to say that it was "a little bit of heaven." And so it was meant to be!

This particular year there are 21 persons in all who will be baptized, confirmed and celebrate first eucharist at the vigil. There are two family groups among that number, with a total of four adults, two infants and five children of school age. As part of the catechumenal process for the unbaptized children of school age, a peer group was formed of children from the parish who were themselves preparing to complete their initiation through the sacraments of confirmation and eucharist. These children in the peer group, baptized in infancy, have journeyed with their young friends from the RCIA process, and now all will complete their initiation together.

In accord with the directives in paragraph 308 of the RCIA, the bishop routinely grants faculties to the pastor to confer confirmation on these children just as he will on those he baptizes. In fact, for several years now, the bishop has allowed a pastoral experiment at St. Lena's whereby for families that request it, all the sacraments of initiation are given to infants in the same ceremony. The practice, common in the church of the East, appears to be catching on and will probably become the "normal" custom eventually.

In the weeks that follow the vigil, the pastor will

do a good many more confirmations and first eucharists for children of the parish. Unless exceptional circumstances prevail, all sacraments of initiation are reserved for the fifty days of Easter. At nearly every Mass throughout this season, youngsters who were baptized in infancy and now are ready to complete their initiation through confirmation and eucharist come forward before the community. A good number of infants are also brought into the church at this time, since it is the normal time of year for all baptisms to be done. While some receive just baptism, other families take advantage of the pastoral experiment and have their infants receive all three sacraments of initiation.

The Liturgy Committee discovered long ago that there was little problem sustaining the joyful momentum of Easter for seven weeks under this system. Every Sunday becomes an echo of Easter joy and a catechesis on the paschal mystery as new members of all ages undergo the sacraments of initiation. The artists who minister to the environment of the worship space still laugh when they think of how their biggest concern used to be keeping fresh flowers on hand. Now, the living symbols of initiation, prominently in evidence, provide an Easter "atmosphere" that is deeply authentic.

There are other symbols that make ritual catechesis of the children so easy at this time of year: the baptismal pool, specially erected in the sanctuary, bubbles with living water for seven weeks. (It's really a modified hot tub, very cleverly disguised; but that is a secret as well kept as the *disciplina arcani* of yesteryear.) The huge decanter of chrism whose perfumed fragrance becomes the familiar smell of Easter gradually empties as week after week its precious oil is lavished upon neophyte after neophyte. The massive Easter candle, handmade by the Over-fifty club, seems to become more impressive each year, as every candle has to be more beautiful than its predecessor. It stands like a gigantic tree trunk or marble column, truly a pillar of fire that makes eyes bulge in wonder on many a child's face. Bread and wine, always fresh baked and lovingly served, whether into the trembling hand of an eight-year-old, or as a drop of wine on the tongue of a squirming infant, becomes the refreshing banquet of salvation for young and old alike. Most important are the living symbols, the newly initiated, and the community that welcomes them.

Ritual catechesis happens almost effortlessly as children are surrounded by and inundated with the mass of initiatory symbolism that "landscapes the religious imagination"[1] of the people of St. Lena's during the great ninety days of Lent-Easter.

PUTTING THE PIECES TOGETHER

What makes possible this marvelous celebration of Christian faith each year at St. Lena's? What are the infrastructures, the pastoral strategies and great ideas that make it all possible? There is little of wizardry, much of sweat, careful planning and organization that is the backdrop to what we have described. There are many "pieces" that have come together over the years, been shaped and reshaped until the "fit" was right, so that a radical vision could flourish and children would be initiated into a vital community of faith.

Like so many of the mega-communities that we call parishes in the United States, St. Lena's came to recognize that its only hope of forming true Christian community on a manageable scale was to implement a small community model throughout the parish. After several grand designs failed, they let it happen naturally; or rather, they nurtured the natural growth of a network which included a variety of small groups. Always holding up the ideal of committed communities that shared faith and life, they welcomed the spontaneous chemistry of every imaginable kind of grouping: neighborhoods, support groups of every species, special interests from scripture study to botany, life-cycle groups that included young adults as well as the senior citizens. A decisive step was taken when official parish structures (committees, councils, and organizations) were also challenged to become communities of sharing on a deeper level.

The ecclesiological vision of the *Order* gradually became the norm for all parish life: the call to and empowerment for ministry happened on a wide scale; scripture-based faith sharing and deep prayer became a regular component of the life of every group; structural processes of healing/conversion were placed at the heart of every parochial involvement; and the turn outward to mission was the *raison d'etre* for it all. A process to welcome newcomers was developed that had tinges of catechumenal-style ministry, with gradual introduction and a progressive call for commitment. The pre-baptismal process for parents of infants became a source of referral to the Returning Catholics Group and a mini-retreat experience in its own right. As the vision of initiation became more well-defined in the parish at large, pre-baptism ministry articulated the same call to conversion. Marriage preparation ministries proliferated and Pre-Cana was replaced by a catechumenal-style process of surprising richness. Newly married couples found support groups available that addressed the joys and stresses of the early years of matrimony, and provided a "mystagogical catechesis" of remarkable vitality.

More and more, since St. Lena's is demographically a "young" community, the focus on family became clear. Family, of course, was conceived broadly to include the gamut of parishioners' living situations. Emphasis on the family as the "domestic church" began to yield significant ramifications across a whole range of parish life. Programming ceased to be divisive of family life and became more inclusive and family-centered. Family enrichment opportunities and services to families in times of stress moved higher on parish agendas. Staff began to resource parents of young children on topics as religious as how to teach children to pray and as mundane as how to parent more effectively.

Another decisive step was taken when the traditional classroom model of religious education was abandoned. For children from infancy through grade six, the parish made a commitment to Christian initiation as it has been described in the pages of this book. The massive transfusion of energy which this brought to the parish's efforts at celebrating its liturgies paid off in ways few dreamed possible. Parents suddenly realized that their child's faith depended on the quality of Sunday worship. Symptomatic of the awakening this triggered was the conversation overheard in the supermarket where one neighbor confronted another over her habit of arriving late and leaving early from Sunday Mass. "It's a bad example for my child," she said, "and undoes everything I'm trying to teach him." End of discussion.

For junior and senior high youngsters, the end of a narrowly conceived classroom-based model of religious education brought a flowering of youth ministry that has become the envy of the diocese. As might be expected, a catechumenal model engaged adults in a new style of youth ministry and called the young people themselves to more extensive peer ministry. An umbrella concept embracing social activities, outreach services, spiritual development experiences and study of the Christian tradition began to integrate formerly disparate elements of youth ministry. Study of the tradition involved peer groups working through a sequence of core requirements and electives from grades seven through twelve, ensuring exposure to a standardized curriculum as well as accommodating the changing interests of age and fashion.

An unexpected benefit of the switch to four- and six-week modules was the great number of new catechists that were attracted by the more focused commitment. Some catechists who became "expert" in the area of their module were used also as part of the RCIA process, where "catechetical households" were being developed to resource those in the catechumenate with special needs or interests. A few of these same folks developed their expertise by forming "study groups" with other interested adults, and some of those groups in turn became part of the parish's network of base communities.

Overall, the contours of parish life at St. Lena's do not immediately stand out as radically different from those of any other parish. They still have an occasional fund-raiser that doubles as a community-building social; they are heavily into both direct service and advocacy for the poor, although their focus is broader than just local issues and needs; they have both Pastoral and Finance Councils, and a sprinkling of committees and organizations (that prefer now to be called ministry teams). To get a feel for the radical vision which is in place at St. Lena's, one has to look closely, listen carefully, and let oneself feel the fervor that is just below the surface.

Though it still hums busily along, the parish has cut out a lot of the peripheral activity that previously consumed so much time and did so little to build God's reign. Parishioners here have busy daily lives, and they recognize that their primary call is to be a leaven in the world, not to spend their life at the parish. Priorities are set here more carefully and more thoughtfully, with an eye to family values in the domestic church. St. Lena's does not qualify yet as a "believer's church," since they are still Roman Catholic enough to welcome anyone and to include on the rolls folks with varying levels of faith and commitment. But there is an unmistakable seriousness of purpose about parish life, a sense of the importance of what they are about.

Sacramental celebrations are still the hub around which all else revolves, but St. Lena's is far from a sacramental service station. Sacraments are linked closely to life experience, and the practical theology surrounding them looks deeply at the meanings of everyday experience. Always there is the call to conversion. Every sacramental celebration in some way or another raises the issue of commitment: commitment to the gospel, to Christian experience lived every day, whether with a newborn infant to rear, with a spouse who shares life most deeply, with the crisis of sickness or death. What is radical about the parishioners of St. Lena's is the awareness of how all that they are and do is rooted in the paschal mystery of Christ.

This is the radical vision into which the children of St. Lena's are initiated. Each Sunday, all year round, they gather to worship with a community that holds dear these values and lovingly passes them on to the next generation. Immersed in a powerful experience of worship and service, and learning to understand and live the Christian faith, the children are formed in a way of life that will endure. Beneath the deceptively ordinary appearance of St. Lena's daily routine, Christians are being made. Young believers of every age whose consciousness has been permeated by the images and meanings of Christ's paschal mystery usher forth into the world from St. Lena's with a mission as radical as their founder's.

Questions for Discussion

1. "The parish . . . a community where belonging and having a sharply defined Catholic identity are strongly held values." How does your parish exhibit a sharply defined Catholic identity?

2. Compare your parish to St. Lena's.

a. What steps would you have to take today to become like it?

b. What are the implications of your taking those steps?

3. The initial premise of this book was that it presented a radical but practical vision for the initiation of children.

a. What have you decided would be most radical in your situation? Why?

b. What is most practical in your situation?

Note

1. Paul Philibert, *Catechumenate*, March, 1989, p. 35.

Annotated Table of Contents

Introduction

1. A New Era

Reflects on the paradigmatic shift in culture and societal structures as a call for a new era in the religious formation of children. Notes the convergence of this shift with the liturgical renewal of Roman Catholic initiatory practice and the demand for a richer Christian experience. Proposes that the task of the new era is *initiation*.

2. Christian Initiation

Sketches the basic characteristics of an initiatory community and the theological contours of the church's initiatory vision as found in the *Order of Christian Initiation of Adults*. Describes the necessary consequences in parish life when the initiation of children becomes a priority.

3. Liturgical Rites

Introduces the concept of ritual catechesis as a constitutive part of the initiation process. Traces the history of the linkage of liturgy and catechesis and applies this tradition to the present-day American parish.

4. A Suitable Pastoral Formation

Explores the catechetical dimensions of #75 of the *Order of Christian Initiation of Adults* as they relate to children of catechetical age. Renegotiates present religious education structures from the viewpoint of lectionary-based catechesis, sponsorship, spiritual direction, and participation in action for justice.

5. Conversion that Is Personal and Developed

Asserts that conversion is at the heart of what a community does when it initiates children. Describes the *Order*'s understanding of conversion and suggests practical applications to the initiation of children in a parish setting. Emphasizes the importance of family-centered and intergenerational catechesis and the development of a personal prayer life.

6. Within the Community of the Faithful

Puts together the pieces of an initiatory vision into a single picture of community life within a typical American parish. Offers a practical model of how a parish arrives at such a vision.